Safe, Seen, and Stretched in the Classroom

Everyone remembers their favorite teacher, but why? What makes some teachers so memorable? Julie Schmidt Hasson spent a year interviewing people about teachers who've shaped their lives, and the result is this captivating book. She shares stories that are both inspirational, highlighting the ways a teacher's actions can make a lasting impact, and also informational, providing models to help teachers make a more consistent impact on the students they serve.

Chapters cover topics such as commitment, vulnerability, power, connection, expectations, community, identity, and equity, while underscoring the importance of making students feel safe, seen, and stretched. In each chapter, the author brings you along as she conducts interviews and hears emotional stories. She also offers practical takeaways and applications for educators of all levels of experience.

With this uplifting book, you will be reminded that your seemingly ordinary interactions in the classroom have extraordinary implications, and that you indeed have the power to influence students' lives – each and every day.

Julie Schmidt Hasson, Ed.D. (@JulieSHasson) is a professor in the Reich College of Education at Appalachian State University. Julie's research on the impact of a teacher is the topic of a TEDx talk and is the focus of her engaging professional development programs. She founded the Chalk and Chances project, a vehicle for elevating and celebrating teachers, in 2017.

T0383663

Safe, Seen, and Stretched in the Classroom

The Remarkable Ways Teachers Shape Students' Lives

Julie Schmidt Hasson

Routledge
Taylor & Francis Group

NEW YORK AND LONDON

First published 2022
by Routledge
605 Third Avenue, New York, NY 10158

and by Routledge
2 Park Square, Milton Park, Abingdon, Oxon OX14 4RN

Routledge is an imprint of the Taylor & Francis Group, an informa business

© 2022 Julie Hasson

Library of Congress Cataloging-in-Publication Data
A catalog record for this title has been requested

ISBN: 978-0-367-64071-2 (hbk)
ISBN: 978-0-367-63464-3 (pbk)
ISBN: 978-1-003-12202-9 (ebk)

DOI: 10.4324/9781003122029

Typeset in Palatino
by Newgen Publishing UK

This book is dedicated to the teacher who raised me and the teacher I raised.

Contents

Acknowledgements

Bringing a book to life is a collaborative process. I am grateful to Lauren Davis and the team at Routledge/Taylor and Francis Group for helping to transform my words into a beautiful book. Thank you to Alison Nissen for shaping this work and to Caite Hamilton for carefully polishing each paragraph.

I've been blessed with unwavering support from my family and friends. Thank you to Brian Hasson for being a partner in every sense of the word and to Cailin Hasson for helping me look at teaching with fresh eyes. Thank you to Laura Estes-Swilley for four decades of friendship and for the hundreds of conversations about what it means to live this teaching life.

Every child deserves to be nurtured as I was (and continue to be). Thank you to my parents, Bob and Gayle Schmidt, who always believed I could be a writer and who proudly displayed every piece on the refrigerator. Thank you to Mrs. Nancy Russell, who encouraged me when I was an emerging reader and again when I was an emerging leader.

I've been lucky enough to spend most of my life surrounded by educators. Thank you to all of the teachers who ignited my love of learning, to my colleagues who keep that fire burning, and to my students who provide my why. Most importantly, thank you to teachers everywhere for making the world a better place by making students feel safe, seen, and stretched every day.

Meet the Author

Dr. Julie Schmidt Hasson is a professor in the Reich College of Education at Appalachian State University. When Julie is not teaching graduate classes in school leadership, she is conducting qualitative research in schools. Julie's research on the impact of a teacher  is the topic of a TEDx talk and is the focus of her engaging professional development programs. She founded the Chalk and Chances project, a vehicle for elevating and celebrating teachers, in 2017. She is also the author of *Unmapped Potential: An Educator's Guide to Lasting Change* (2017). Julie's mother and grandmother were both teachers, and she is the proud mother of a teacher. She lives in Boone, North Carolina, with her husband, two dogs, and several geese.

Introduction

Just the mention of Nancy Russell's name elicits a rush of emotions, a mix of gratitude, wonder, and joy. Mrs. Russell was my first grade teacher, and she forever changed the way I see myself as a learner. Everything I have achieved has been built on the foundation she laid. Mrs. Russell retired in the summer of 2015, the same year I accepted an assistant professor position at Florida Southern College. In addition to teaching graduate students, I needed to identify a focus for my research. I became interested (more like obsessed) with a big question: what do teachers like Mrs. Russell say and do to make a lasting impact on students' lives?

To answer this question I needed to interview former students. It turns out that people who had once been students are everywhere. So, I positioned myself at farmers' markets, flea markets, craft fairs, and college campuses with a sign inviting these former students to talk with me about their teachers. Although this was not my usual method of data collection, it has yielded a deep understanding of teacher impact. The stories participants shared have made the abstract concept of teacher impact more concrete.

I used a grounded theory approach to data collection and analysis, simultaneously collecting, coding, and analyzing data from my interviews and field notes. I did not purposefully select participants for the study. Instead, I placed myself where I was likely to find a diversity of backgrounds and perspectives. I made no assumptions about the race, ethnicity, gender, economic status, or ability of the participants. In some cases, information

DOI: 10.4324/9781003122029-1

about these identities was shared in their stories. I chose not to use an audio recorder in data collection, but instead, I recorded notes, quotes, and observations in my journal.

The stories participants shared are inspirational, highlighting the ways a teacher's actions and interactions in the classroom can make a lasting impact on a student's life. And the stories are also informational, providing models to help teachers make a more consistent impact on the students they serve. As I continued to collect stories and the amount of data grew, themes emerged. It became clear that in the classrooms of their most impactful teachers, people remembered feeling safe, seen, and stretched. My findings indicate that a teacher's impact is centered in the way the teacher connects with students and what the teacher expects of students.

The book you are holding represents a synthesis of the findings after the first year of the project. The names of some of the participants (and other identifying information) have been changed to protect confidentiality. In some cases, the timeline was compressed and events reordered to assist the reader in following the narrative. It is important to note that all memories are reconstructions. The stories people tell are filtered through their current realities. The meaning given to a story is influenced by the events that have transpired since the experience. I have reported the stories as they were told to me (with a bit of editing for readability). I have reported the events to the best of my recollection, with support from my field notes.

In the pages of this book, I situated my findings in the context of existing research on teaching and learning. My goal was to create a work grounded in evidence but also accessible to teachers. I continually find myself straddling two worlds, with one foot in the scholarly realm and the other foot in the classroom. This research has deepened my affinity for teachers and their profession. This work has affirmed my belief that teachers have the power to shape students' lives, and they do so in a million different ways every day. The seemingly ordinary actions and interactions that occur in classrooms have extraordinary implications. I offer this book as a token of gratitude to the teachers who shaped my life and as a love letter to the profession that continues to captivate me.

1

Lessons on Commitment

The influence of our teachers is indelibly woven into the fabric of our lives. I let this truth wash over me like the afternoon sun as I stood in the street with Ellen. We met just three minutes ago, but now her hands were holding mine. I bent down to look her in the eyes, paying little attention to the other patrons at the farmers' market as they dug through the bins in the booths surrounding us, picking out peppers and avocados. Halfway through her story, I felt a warm tear roll down my cheek. At the beginning of this project, I would strain to hold back my emotions as people revealed such personal memories. I believed the detached stance of a researcher would serve the project well. Now, nearly a year and 276 stories later, I have realized the futility of suppressing my feelings. And, most importantly, I have come to appreciate pants with pockets big enough to hold a pack of tissues.

When this particular stranger approached on her motorized scooter, she first caught the attention of my husband, Brian, who patiently knelt down to tell her about the project. Happy to let him answer questions, I packed away the banner and folding table. The market was closing, the temperature was rising, and I was shutting down. I could feel the heat of the brick street through my sandals, and I wished I could teleport myself out of the crowd. I'm an introvert, and I typically have five good hours of story-collecting before I hit my wall. Brian, whose emotional batteries stay charged much longer than mine, believes in

DOI: 10.4324/9781003122029-2

pushing past walls, so I wasn't surprised when he waved me over. "This is Ellen," he said. "You need to talk with her."

I forced a smile as I took his place. Ellen removed her straw hat, fluffed her silver curls, and took my hands in hers. Her firm grip betrayed her bony, crooked fingers. "I need to tell you about my high school speech teacher," she began. "It's been almost 70 years since I last saw him, but I never forgot him." I was sure she could not possibly remember details from her school experience, but I was wrong.

Ellen continued, "Mr. Dillon was a legend in our town, a gifted orator and longtime speech teacher. He seemed invincible, until he announced his throat cancer diagnosis. He promised students he would return after treatment." Eventually, Ellen explained, Mr. Dillon did return to school—but he was almost unrecognizable. He was alarmingly thin, and a tracheostomy left him with a hole in his neck. He had to hold a microphone near his throat in order to speak. "At first, the students were a little uneasy," she admitted. "It was difficult to focus on what he was saying as he struggled to get the words out. But after a while, we all got used to it. He was just Mr. Dillon again."

I asked Ellen about the lasting impact Mr. Dillon had made on her life. She paused for a moment before answering. "I have experienced many challenges over the years since I was in Mr. Dillon's speech class. When I start to feel sorry for myself, I remember the way he showed up every day, fully committed to teaching. Mr. Dillon has been my model of perseverance and strength. He is proof that it is possible to keep moving forward, even when obstacles get in the way. I appreciate how much he taught me—about giving a speech and about living a purposeful life."

"Wow," was the only response I could summon. In Ellen's eyes I could still see traces of that young girl from Mr. Dillon's speech class. While sharing the memory of her high school days, she became animated and lively. I felt strangely connected to this woman I met only minutes before. We talked a bit longer, then she squeezed my hands one more time and I watched as she disappeared into the crowd.

I was struck by the lesson Ellen had carried for almost seven decades. The most powerful lesson Mr. Dillon taught was not about grammar or diction; his life was his greatest teaching tool. Although he was a speech teacher, his actions spoke much louder than his words. The gift of the story left me re-energized. I felt grateful, and I couldn't wait to add it to the collection, certain it would provide insight into the lasting impact teachers make on their students' lives.

Early Inspiration

It's my curiosity about teacher impact that led me to collect these stories in the first place. In fact, the origin of this project likely goes back to my own childhood. It was the morning of September 8, 1975, and I was standing outside a heavy blue door. My 6-year-old heart was beating fast. It was my first day of first grade, and (as my academically gifted older brother kept reminding me), I was not yet a reader and thus not ready for the challenges waiting on the other side of that door. Just when I decided to run back to my old kindergarten classroom, the door opened and out stepped a beautiful young woman with long, straight, brown hair. She was an angel in a sage-colored bell bottom pantsuit. I clutched my new Holly Hobbie lunchbox and peered up at her through my fringe of blonde bangs. With a reassuring smile, she guided me inside. Her name was Nancy Russell, and her impact on my life is undeniable.

I came to love everything about first grade. I clearly remember the easel with cups of thick paint and fat brushes in the tray. I can still picture Mrs. Russell setting the needle of the record player down on a spinning vinyl disc to play Carole King singing "Chicken Soup with Rice." That year, with considerable patience and diligence on Mrs. Russell's part, this dyslexic and highly anxious kid became a reader. I could believe in myself because my teacher believed in me. Looking back, I realize that if she had shown frustration or doubt instead of comfort and confidence, I would have seen myself differently as a learner.

The following year, I started second grade with a new attitude and a new lunch box … Charlie's Angels. My confidence had grown and I felt like I belonged in school. Eventually, I became a teacher, just like Mrs. Russell, playing "Chicken Soup with Rice" on the CD player for my own students. After 20 years of teaching, I became a principal. I even had the unexpected privilege of being Mrs. Russell's principal for a few years, but that's another story for another day.

By the time Mrs. Russell retired in 2015, I had accepted a position as an assistant professor in the School of Education at my alma mater, Florida Southern College. My beloved teacher's retirement led me to contemplate how some teachers leave a legacy of impact. Everything I achieved was built on the foundation Mrs. Russell laid, and there were hundreds of others like me. Her students became teachers, doctors, and parents, and our performance in all of those roles was colored by what we experienced under her care. I began to wonder if everyone had a Mrs. Russell. As a new professor, I was expected to research important phenomena in my field. I could think of no better topic to explore than the lasting impact of a teacher on students' lives, but I wasn't sure how to tackle it or even where to start. So, I did what I always do when I struggle with a big idea: I called my best friend, Laura, and asked her to meet me for lunch.

Teacher Talk

Laura slid into the booth across from me and dropped her red leather tote on the bench. "What's going on?"

"I'm thinking about a research project, and I need to think it out loud with you."

Laura stirred some sweetener into her iced tea and settled in. "Hit me with it."

"I want to find out about teacher impact. What is it? Can we measure it?"

"You mean like how much students learn? How what we teach helps them in the future?"

"Sort of. You've been teaching high school English for almost 20 years. What do you think your impact has been on students?"

Laura sat back and looked at the ceiling. "It's hard to say. I know what I *hope* my impact is. And my former students sometimes reach out to share something they have remembered or used from my class. I guess that's really my only evidence."

"So, you're saying unless former students reach out, teachers don't really know their long-term impact?"

She nodded. "Yes, it's hard for us to know."

"It seems I won't get too far asking *teachers* about their impact."

"That is going to be tough for you," Laura said through a smirk. "Everybody you know is a teacher."

I had to admit she was right. If I wanted to find out about teacher impact, I'd need to go outside my circle, and my friend knew how challenging that would be for me, an avowed introvert.

"How about you?" I asked, "Was there a teacher who shaped your life?" It struck me that in our 40 years of friendship, I had never asked Laura this question.

She stirred her tea again, pausing before responding. "I suppose Judi Briant was the teacher who uncovered my gifts. You remember what I was like in high school. I had little interest in academics and a solid reputation as a party girl, but Mrs. Briant somehow saw past that. She figured out what interested me and offered it up in an engaging way. She hooked me with *The Great Gatsby*," Laura said. "The portrait of a generation obsessed with fun and unconcerned with consequences spoke to me. Beyond the themes, Mrs. Briant helped me see the grace and elegance of Fitzgerald's writing. All I wanted to do was write like that."

Laura described Mrs. Briant's class as the one place she felt smart, and she defined her beloved English teacher as the one who inspired her to write. She still counts her as a mentor and a model. She said, "Mrs. Briant made me want to do exactly what she was doing. I try to channel her passionate presence in my own classroom every day."

Laura and I had many of the same teachers, and I remembered Mrs. Briant fondly, too. "You know," I admitted, "I calculated that we spent around 16,000 hours in school and probably had over 40 different teachers. Much of those hours are a blur for me, and I can't recall many of the names and faces of our teachers."

"Same here," Laura agreed. "Much of it is a haze, but a few of those teachers, like Mrs. Briant, stand out. Why do you think we still remember some of them so clearly?"

"It's a mystery to me. I can't help but wonder what made them so memorable. What did they say and do that stuck with us for all of these years? I guess that's what I hope to discover."

As I waved goodbye to Laura and pulled out of the restaurant's parking lot, I tried to remember the teachers who stood in front of us during our high school years. I could picture some in clear detail. I recalled every book I read in Mr. Resciniti's literature class and every project completed in home economics with Mrs. Khan. They taught different subjects and each had a unique teaching style, yet there were commonalities. I knew it had something to do with the way they all made me feel, but I couldn't articulate it yet.

A Persistent Narrative

While driving home, I considered what teaching was like in the 1980s. Although Laura and I were unaware at the time, a significant event impacted our teachers in 1983. Ronald Reagan's Secretary of Education, Terrel Bell, convened a commission to investigate his suspicions about the quality of education in the United States. He believed students were falling behind other nations, and his commission found data to support his hunches. The average score of all students who took the SAT had dropped from the 1960s to the 1980s. In addition, students in the United States did not rank first (or even second) in any of 19 selected tests of academic achievement when compared with other industrialized nations.

Bell's commission drafted a report, *A Nation at Risk: The Imperative for Educational Reform*, which was widely publicized.

Amidst the Cold War and a recession, the report stoked fears about the vulnerability of the United States to threats from other countries. The narrative of failing schools and rampant mediocrity in education began. The report was the subject of evening news stories and landed on the front page of newspapers. In the month following the report's release, *The Washington Post* alone published two dozen stories about it. Teacher blaming, shaming, and criticism became the focus of pundits and politicians. But if our teachers felt the sting of that storyline, it was never apparent to us. Mrs. Briant, Mr. Resciniti, Mrs. Khan, and their colleagues still showed up fully committed to teaching us every day with undeniable enthusiasm.

The narrative instigated by *A Nation at Risk* persists to this day, despite evidence to the contrary. Seven years after the release of the report, Admiral James Watkins, the Secretary of Energy, sought more information as part of an education initiative. He commissioned the Sandia Laboratories in New Mexico to look more deeply into the data on which *A Nation at Risk* was based. The scientists at Sandia examined the data from every angle. They found that when they disaggregated it into subgroups (based on characteristics such as gender, race, and economic status), nearly every subgroup held steady or improved from the 1960s to the 1980s. So, how could overall average scores have dropped? How could it have appeared that our nation's students were falling behind?

The scientists found the answer in Simpson's Paradox, which shows the average can change in one direction while the subgroups change in the opposite direction if proportions among the subgroups change. They realized that it was mainly students from privileged backgrounds that participated in the SAT during the 1960s. At that time, test-takers were mostly white, economically advantaged students who had access to tutors and other support. However, by the 1980s, college became a possibility for a larger and more diverse set of students. SAT examinees in the 1980s had expanded to a broader population, and the proportion of wealthy test-takers had decreased. The *Sandia Report* decreed schools were not failing. In fact, educators accomplished something remarkable: expanding educational opportunities for all students.

When the *Sandia Report* was completed, the federal government buried it. Many months later, once it was finally released, it did not get the same kind of publicity as *A Nation at Risk* had. It was mainly discussed in academic journals. The narrative of failing schools remains a powerful political tool, and it drives educational reform policy to this day. However, the trends uncovered by the scientists at Sandia have held. There is still much work to do—not every child in every school is being served well. But despite rising child poverty rates and lack of adequate funding in many states, the education system in the United States has produced steady results.

Sweet Revelations

Lost in my thoughts about teachers, I pulled into the driveway after lunch. I walked up the old, brick steps of our bungalow and went straight into the den to capture my conversation with Laura in my journal. The afternoon sun refracted light through the glass apple on my desk and formed a rainbow on the wall. The glass apple is one of my most treasured belongings. It was passed down to me from my mother when she retired from a 30-year teaching career. Looking at the shining apple, I thought about my mom and about Mrs. Russell. What did it mean, all those days spent with students? Teaching had not bestowed riches or acclaim, but perhaps they were left with something more deeply satisfying.

Nationally, teachers earn 19% less than similarly skilled and educated professionals, a discrepancy that has been increasing over the past two decades. In his book, *Schoolteacher*, Dan Lortie examines the limited opportunities for upward movement in salary and position that accompany a career in teaching. Starting pay is reasonable, but pay increases are smaller percentages of the base salary as teachers remain longer in the profession. And unlike other professions, monetary incentives are not based on variations in effort and talent. Instead, teachers typically cite psychic rewards as their reason for continuing the work. They describe the deep satisfaction in knowing they have influenced a student. And, just as most students carry the memory of a teacher who impacted their lives, most teachers cherish the memories of accomplishments with students.

My dogs, Winnie and Charlie, competed for room at my feet while I sat at my desk and thought about how I felt in Mrs. Russell's classroom. I reflected on the way my graduate students react when I ask them to talk about their favorite teachers. They light up like the apple on my desk. It seems that just saying the names of teachers we love conjures up inexplicable gratitude and joy. I once heard author Kurt Vonnegut say that being in the presence of his favorite teacher made him prouder to be human and happier to be alive. Surely the greatest reward for a life spent teaching is to be remembered that way.

The barking of Winnie and Charlie pulled me out of my thoughts, signaling that Brian was home. He came into the den and looked over my shoulder. "How's it going?"

I turned to look up at him. "Can I ask you something?"

He winked. "It depends."

"Is there a teacher you remember? Not just the teacher's name, but specific things about him or her."

He pulled up a chair and thought for a minute. "Mrs. Robinson. She was my seventh grade English teacher."

"What do you remember about her? What did she say or do that stuck with you?"

Brian leaned back in his chair, and shared a story I'd never heard before.

"My mom and I moved from a small, rural town in south New Jersey to the Miami area two weeks before I started seventh grade," he said. "It was a culture shock. I entered school on that first day knowing just one other kid. I felt awkward and alone, like a complete outsider. My day improved the minute I entered Mrs. Robinson's English class. She wore a bright, floral-patterned dress. The only thing brighter than her dress was her smile. She immediately made me feel safe and happy."

Brian looked forward to being in Mrs. Robinson's class every day. When he felt like a nobody, she made him feel like a some-body. He said, "She used to call me her 'Right-hand Man.' When I turned in papers, she wrote positive comments in brightly colored felt tip pens. She boosted my confidence and gave me a sense of belonging." Brian couldn't explain why he remembered her so well; there were no big dramatic moments of impact. He simply remembered her positive energy. "As students," he explained, "we knew she was happy to be teaching us."

Brian and I had spent 30 years sharing stories, but this was the first I heard about Mrs. Robinson. I suddenly saw the young, insecure kid from Jersey still living inside this man I knew so well. We were both professors—why had we never talked about our own teachers? Hearing Brian's story made me wonder who else had a story yet unknown to me. I wondered if asking about a favorite teacher might reveal unseen parts of the other people in my life.

I began asking my family, friends, and closest colleagues about their teachers, and had the same experience every time. People I had known for decades revealed stories about the ways teachers shaped their lives. They admitted they hadn't thought about their teachers in years, but prompted by my question, the memories came rushing back. I was on to something interesting. I became determined to explore this phenomenon of lasting teacher impact, but first I needed a plan.

Research Design

In the scholarly realm, we call it research design. I'm trained in qualitative research, gathering data through interviews and observations, which I suppose makes me a professional story collector. Typically, I identify specific participants who fit my criteria, gain their consent to participate in my study, audio tape and transcribe lengthy interviews about the topic, and analyze the data. But my usual approach was not going to work for this project. It would require some adjustments. I needed to meet with Hank.

Hank Lance oversees the Institutional Review Board at my college. No research happens without going through Hank. His official task is to ensure ethical standards and protect the welfare of participants in human subject research, but lucky for me, he has expanded his role far beyond that. Hank's background is in experimental research, but his natural curiosity and open mind draw him into discussions about all types of research questions. It was an unusually chilly March morning in Lakeland when I walked across campus to find him in his office. I explained my dilemma. He leaned back in his chair and scratched his head. "What exactly are you trying to find out?"

"I want to know what teachers say and do to make a lasting impact on students."

Hank paused before asking, "Who do you need to interview?'

"Former students, I suppose—people who attended K-12 schools."

He grinned. "Those people are not hard to find."

"That's the challenge." I shifted in my seat. "They're everywhere, but how will I know which ones have a story? And, how will I get them to share that story with me?"

Hank thought for a moment. "You just need to put yourself where people congregate. You need a visual to tell them why you're there and invite them to participate."

"Like a sign?"

Hank laughed. "Okay, a sign, but worded in a concise and friendly way. No research jargon."

"So, I go to public places and put out my sign. What about consent? I am inviting them to have brief conversations. I can't spend 10 minutes explaining a long consent form."

Hank helped me draft a shortened consent form and approved my research design, but the challenge was just beginning. As I walked back across the campus and the two blocks home, it hit me: the study Hank and I designed did not exactly draw upon my natural strengths and tendencies. Although qualitative research is always a bit unpredictable, I tend to create a highly structured plan. Typically, I carefully identify and screen participants who fit the criteria of my study and judiciously craft a series of interview questions. This study would rely on inviting complete strangers to respond to one open-ended (and very personal) question. My nervous stomach started churning.

Critical Shortage

At 3:00 a.m., my eyes were wide open and my mind was racing, a regular occurrence. Next to me in bed, Brian was snoring. Winnie and Charlie were snoring. I found it strangely soothing—it reminded me that sleep is possible. I was still thinking about my visit with Hank, but I was also worrying over the plight of the principal of my neighborhood elementary school. She called that afternoon to ask if I knew any prospective teachers. Two of her faculty members were going on medical leave soon and she had no candidates to fill those vacancies. Unfortunately, her plight was becoming common. Many students in my central Florida district were being taught by substitutes or in combined classes due to a growing teacher shortage. It was discomforting to realize how many students might not get to experience the impact of a Mrs. Russell.

Most of the teachers Laura and I admired in the 1980s retired after long careers. During their tenure, they witnessed significant shifts in the profession. Educational researcher Richard Ingersoll led a team in examining trends over the past three decades. The researchers found the teaching force had become less experienced and less stable. When Laura and I graduated in 1987, the average teacher had 15 years of experience. Now, the average is less than five years. Experience matters in teaching as effectiveness increases over the first several years of practicing teaching. With experience, teachers become better at dealing with student behavior and helping students with diverse needs. The lack of veterans also means a lack of mentors to support and coach the beginners, and this guidance is critical. Students are the biggest losers when teacher turnover is high.

Ingersoll and his team uncovered another trend. By 2016, more than 44% of teachers were leaving the profession within the first five years. Unfortunately, this trend continues. No doubt low teacher salaries are a factor in many states, but teachers cite other reasons for leaving. Lack of autonomy and little discretion over the decisions impacting their students are sources of frustration. Lack of resources and services for students also contributes to burnout and attrition. Turnover is greatest in high-poverty schools, where teachers feel ill-equipped to meet the wide-ranging needs of their students, and the number of high-poverty schools has dramatically increased over the past three decades.

Professional Commitment

I continued to fidget with the blankets while contemplating the convergence of factors leading to this critical teacher shortage. I finally gave up and went to make myself a cup of tea. I walked into the den and looked at the apple on my desk and thought about my mom. She, and others who spent a lifetime in schools, understood the importance of commitment, like Ellen's Mr. Dillon, who pushed aside the pain of cancer recovery to face the students in front of him. I remembered Mrs. Briant and her colleagues who shook off the painful narrative of failure and never let it impact their teaching. And surely Brian's Mrs. Robinson had bad days, but any change in her mood was never evident to him. I realized they shared a characteristic common to all great teachers: professional commitment.

Professional commitment has been defined as a willing-ness to put forth considerable effort, beyond what is contrac-tually obligated. Teachers with a high degree of professional commitment feel a sense of identity tied to their work, a sense of meaning in their work, and a sense of responsibility toward the profession's problems and challenges. Researchers have con-sistently found a correlation between professional commitment and effective instruction. Teachers who give discretionary effort (going above and beyond) perform better and produce better outcomes for students. It's not surprising that we would remember those teachers who were professionally committed and invested in our success.

Perhaps teaching at its core is about commitment, about being dedicated to the cause of students' development. It's about put-ting aside pain, pride, and self-protection to prioritize the needs of students. It's about a never-ending quest to become better at meeting those needs. I decided the least I could do, despite my discomfort, was commit to this project. So later that day, I drove to the print shop to order a sign.

Applying Lessons on Commitment

When I began this project, I knew I would gain a deeper understanding of teacher impact. What I could not have predicted was the way the project helped me become a better teacher for my graduate students. Identifying professional commitment as a theme in the stories led me to reflect on my own level of commitment and led me to dive into the literature on this topic. I knew that knowledge alone would not transform my teaching; so, I found ways to apply what I learned. Below are three areas of focus related to professional commitment. Within each area are practices and questions for reflection to help you stay longer and be stronger for your students.

Area 1: Finding Meaning in the Work

Think about the connection between your day-to-day tasks and personal values.

What is the deeper meaning in your work and how can you intentionally connect that meaning with the small actions you take each day?

Consider the impact of your work in a larger context.

How does your work impact the world beyond your class-room and school?

Area 2: Seeking Opportunities for Growth

Seek professionally relevant knowledge and try new strategies in the classroom when you need to shake up routines that are becoming too comfortable.

What do you learn about your students and yourself in the process of trying something new?

Noticing improvement is a way to increase motivation and deepen professional commitment, and recognizing your own development can be deeply satisfying.

How do you recognize and celebrate your own growth?

Area 3: Seeking Feedback

Putting forth a high level of effort is especially rewarding when accompanied by feedback that indicates the effort is worthwhile.

How do you identify the ways your actions are tied to students' learning and growth?

An open-ended question, an honest discussion, or a simple survey at the end of a lesson can help you improve and become even more committed.

What kind of student feedback can you seek to increase your professional growth and commitment?

Notes and Works Cited

p. 8   *A nation at risk : the imperative for educational reform : A report to the Nation and the Secretary of Education, United States Department of Education*. (1983). National Commission on Excellence in Education.

p. 9   Carson, C. C., Huelskamp, R. M., & Woodall, T. D. (1993). Perspectives on education in America. *The Journal of Educational Research*, *86*(5), 259–310.

p. 10   Allegretto, S. & Lawrence M. (2018). The teacher penalty has hit a new high. *Economic Policy Institute*, September 5, 2018.

p. 10   Lortie, D. C. (1975). *Schoolteacher; a sociological study*. University of Chicago Press.

p. 11   Vonnegut, K. (2004). *The shape of a story*. The Case College Scholars Program Lecture. Retrieved from https://www.youtube.com/watch?v=GOGru_4z1Vc

p. 14   Ingersoll, R. M. (2001). Teacher turnover and teacher shortages: An organizational analysis. *American Educational Research Journal*, *38*(3), 499–534.

p. 15   Firestone, W. A., & Pennell, J. R. (1993). Teacher commitment, working conditions, and differential incentive policies. *Review of Educational Research*, *63*(4), 489–525.

2

Lessons on Vulnerability

I headed out around Lake Morton toward downtown. I always drive slowly around the lake to get a look at the swans; the strong breeze had them bobbing on the water like fluffy little boats. I love living in Lakeland, but I didn't always feel great affection for this place. When I was little my grandparents lived here, and we visited them every Sunday. Back then, I found the slow pace exasperating. The town seemed old, and so did the people.

I remember thinking that there were two kinds of older people living in Lakeland. One seemed constantly irritated and troubled, moving like their bodies were full of wet sand. They were the ones at the pool in my grandparents' mobile home park who complained that the grandkids were too noisy, that we splashed too much, or weren't wearing the requisite swim caps. The other kind seemed lighter, still fascinated with the world and happy to be in the presence of children. My grandmother was one of the lighter ones. She always loved to watch kids play. I wonder if it made her miss the years she spent teaching.

I drove past the pavilion on the lake, the place where I went on a first date with Brian when we were students at the college down the road (the same college where we both now teach). I've grown to appreciate the beauty of the old buildings and brick streets of Lakeland. And I've grown to love the eclectic mix of people who fill downtown for the farmers' market, a food truck rally, or Fourth of July fireworks. I have come to understand why my grandmother loved this small city.

DOI: 10.4324/9781003122029-3

A Sign

Once downtown, I parked on a side street and walked into our local print shop. Justin, whom I recognized from previous visits, greeted me from behind the counter, his carefully coiffed hair a contrast to his bushy beard and faded Metallica t-shirt. I tried to explain what I needed while Justin tilted his head and pushed up his glasses.

"Let me get this straight—you need a sign for your research project?"

"Yes," I said, leaning on the counter. "Something I can stick in the ground by my table to invite people to stop and talk with me."

"I see," Justin nodded. "Like a corrugated plastic sign you could slide on to a metal stake. What do you want on your sign?"

I thought for a minute. "It needs to be simple and welcoming. Maybe something like, *Tell me about a teacher who made an impact.*"

Justin considered my idea. "I'm not sure what you mean by impact and, no offense, but it sounds a little academic."

We agreed on a phrase with a friendlier tone: *Let's chat about a teacher you remember.*

As Justin was writing up the order, he began to tell me about his favorite teacher, Mrs. Downey. He remembered her seventh grade language arts classroom as a safe place. "Middle school was a challenging time. I was small and struggled academically, which made me feel insecure. I avoided anything that would potentially draw attention or cause me embarrassment," Justin began. "Mrs. Downey's reading class was mostly boys. I had known many of them since elementary school when we were all diagnosed with learning disabilities. After years of teasing, we learned to hide behind protective armor. We ascribed to the *'attack them before they attack you'* philosophy."

When the boys arrived in Mrs. Downey's classroom the first day, Justin said, they were surprised to find two guinea pigs. At first there was some eye-rolling and groaning, "We were clearly too cool for class pets," Justin admitted. But little did they know that George and Lennie, as they were named, had the power to break through the armor of middle school boys. "Most of us were reluctant to read out loud, but we were willing to read to George or Lennie." As he relayed the memory, Justin acknowledged the brilliance of Mrs. Downey's plan. "When I felt unworthy, she gave me responsibility for the guinea pigs' care. When I felt unlovable, Lennie and George loved me unconditionally. When I armored up, they softened my heart. I took risks as a learner that I would not have taken in any other class."

I was surprised at Justin's willingness to share such a personal story. I had been to the print shop a few times before, but I would not have described us as more than acquaintances until this moment. Knowing this piece of his history made me feel more connected to the young man behind the counter. Justin and I represented different generations, but we had much in common. His description of struggle and insecurity took me right back to the big blue door on my first day of first grade. Mrs. Russell had her hands full with me, just as Mrs. Downey did with Justin.

We all have a need for social belonging, for feeling connected, and our fear of rejection creates a sensitivity to the responses of others. This sensitivity may be heightened for stigmatized groups of students, those who have learning challenges, live in economic instability, or come from historically excluded populations. Researchers Claude Steele and Joshua Aronson call this threat of being judged by a societal generalization a "stereotype threat." The anxiety of confirming a negative stereotype can impact a student's performance or even willingness to attempt a task. A close, trusting relationship with a teacher and a safe classroom culture can significantly mitigate the effects of stereotype threat.

Education activist, William Ayers, advocates viewing each student as a unique and multifaceted being who lives and learns in idiosyncratic ways. He urges teachers to resist labels, generalizations, or anything else that ignores this individuality. No doubt teachers like Mrs. Russell and Mrs. Downey look at students through the curious eyes and generous hearts that Ayers describes. They see the inherent value and complexity in every student. When I started this project, I committed to seeing the people I encountered as three-dimensional beings with unique histories, perspectives, and values. True vulnerability requires bringing our own complex and messy selves into connection and relationship with other complex, messy selves. That's exactly what happened in the print shop between Justin and me.

Vulnerability and Growth

On the drive back to campus, I thought more about Justin and his protective walls. As teachers, we ask students to take risks—both learning and connecting require it. So does sharing an idea or something we've created. Some students have experienced pain from this risk often enough that they withdraw. Like Justin, they choose to armor themselves rather than reveal their weaknesses. Unfortunately, the walls they build to protect themselves hinder learning and rob them of the joy found in growth and connection.

Vulnerability is a complex and multifaceted emotional experience that can occur in different contexts. A person's willingness to be in a state of vulnerability is influenced by perceptions of the situation, sense of identity, beliefs, values, and sense of competence. If teachers can create classroom conditions that help students feel safe, competent, and supported, students are more likely to open themselves to the possibility of potential risk. But students must also understand why taking down their armor and opening up is important. Researcher and author, Brene Brown, describes vulnerability as uncertainty, risk, and emotional exposure. She also calls vulnerability the birthplace of joy, belonging, courage, empathy, and growth. Being vulnerable is necessary for learning, as all change and growth is accompanied by risk. Perhaps our most challenging job as educators is to help students value learning and growth enough that the satisfaction of it is worth the risk.

The classroom can be a precarious place. Answering a question, offering an opinion, or sharing an idea risks potential embarrassment, ridicule, and rejection. Just as people like Justin shared beautiful, affirming moments in classrooms with me, people also shared moments of humiliation and shame. When fear is driving students to protect themselves, they armor up.

Even the students most eager to learn will not open up in a classroom that feels emotionally unsafe. This closed stance inhibits learning, connection, and collaboration. Being disengaged makes a student's experience in a classroom unmemorable, but being humiliated or shamed makes a classroom experience painfully memorable. I knew that I wanted to create memorable moments in my classroom, but I suddenly felt a great responsibility for the kinds of memories my students would carry.

I considered vulnerability as I arrived on campus and walked into the education building to teach my graduate class. I opened by telling my students about the research project I was launching. They asked questions and talked about the teachers they remembered. Like me, many of them became educators because of the impact that a teacher had on their lives, and I wondered out loud if we chose to teach in an effort to recapture the way we felt in our favorite teachers' classrooms. We also talked about painful memories and the way those inform our choices. We all agreed that the teachers we remember influence the beliefs we carry about teaching and the way we relate to our own students.

After class, one of my students approached and asked if she could tell me about a teacher who impacted her life. Beth had a clear memory of a powerful moment with Mrs. Rivers, her first grade teacher. "I was in first grade when my older brother was killed in an accident," Beth said. "I was devastated and felt sure I could never be happy again. I had been out of school for a week when Mrs. Rivers knocked on our door."

Beth explained how the teacher came in quietly, sat down in the living room next to her student, and placed a plastic milk jug on the table. Beth took a peek inside and saw a stick with one green leaf, a gray-green chrysalis hanging from it.

Beth remembers exactly what Mrs. Rivers said: 'This butterfly is not in a good place right now. It's going to struggle for a while. But then, it will be stronger and more beautiful than ever. You will, too.' "

Beth kept the jug and watched for two weeks until, finally, the chrysalis began to shake and out came a beautiful butterfly. It flapped its wet wings and climbed onto the stick. Later that day, she took it outside to let it fly free. Beth said, "Mrs. Rivers was right; I started to feel better. Things would never be the same, but I would learn to cope. I have carried that lesson through every struggle since."

Beth had been sitting in front of me for months, but I had been missing this important piece of her history. I realized how little I really knew about her, or my other students. Their professional roles, as well as their strengths and struggles, were familiar to me; I could even recall the names of some of their family members. But there was still so much to discover. Talking about their former teachers elicited one of the most significant and reflective conversations of the semester. A deeper understanding of each other and of ourselves as teachers and learners came out of that discussion.

Professional Vulnerability

After class, I walked to my office and sat in the leather armchair I keep in the corner. I had been thinking about vulnerability and risk since my conversation with Justin earlier in the day. Beth's story gave me even more to ponder. It must have taken an immense amount of courage for Mrs. Rivers to walk into a home teeming with grief and suffering. I thought about what I would have done, sent a card or maybe flowers. I might have called on the phone, hoping it would go to voicemail so I could leave a quick message of sympathy. I would have missed the pain, but I would also have missed the opportunity to teach a lesson that a little girl would carry and use for a lifetime, to comfort a family in a way that only being present can do.

For many educators (me included), our sense of identity is wrapped up in our sense of competence as teachers. Risking that feeling of proficiency feels scary. One of the most beautiful traits of great teachers is the willingness to put aside personal comfort for students' needs. Teachers like Mrs. Rivers open themselves to the possibility of embarrassment, loss, or emotional pain because they believe their students benefit from this openness. Trying to connect with a student or trying a new instructional strategy in the classroom poses a risk to our sense of competence. But courage is contagious, and the most powerful tool for increasing vulnerability in the classroom is our own modeling.

I was suddenly seized with the realization that my new research project would require breaking down my walls and showing up with the vulnerability necessary for connection. Asking people to remember school experiences would no doubt bring up emotions—both welcome and unwanted. But I knew that acknowledging my uncertainty and moving forward could inspire my students to be more professionally vulnerable. Despite my fears, I felt ready. I knew what I needed to do, but I wasn't sure where to go first. I called Laura to generate some ideas. She picked up right away with her usual greeting: "Hey, what's up?"

"I have a plan. I ordered a sign. Now I just need to figure out where to go. I want to start small."

Laura paused for a moment. "You know, my high school is hosting a craft fair next week. I think there are still open spots. There will probably be a big enough crowd to get some participants but not big enough to overwhelm you." I registered for a booth before I changed my mind.

Risky Business

A week later, I picked up the sign from Justin and went home to pack the car for the craft fair. I slid a folding table, two chairs, and the sign in the back. As I was closing the hatch, I saw my neighbor, Jill, approaching. Jill is a first grade teacher, so we chatted about some new policies impacting our local school district. Then I told her about my project.

Jill's eyes widened. "I love what you're doing! It'll help us all remember what it felt like to be a student," she said. "I had so many great teachers. Now you have me thinking about the ones who influenced me."

I asked Jill to tell me about one of those teachers who made a lasting impact on her life and she told me about Mr. Christie, her high school history teacher.

"As the '70s were turning into the '80s, I was turning into a teenage activist. I adored Mr. Christie's radical hippie vibe," Jill told me. "Armed with facts, statistics, and informed opinions, he loved to debate his students." Jill remembered watching *The Nightly News* one evening and becoming aware of the starvation in Cambodia. The next day in Mr. Christie's class, she raised her hand to ask why it was happening and why our country wasn't doing more to help. "I watched Mr. Christie pause for a moment, stroke his beard, and consider how to respond," Jill said. "Then he put down his lesson plan and textbook, pulled down all of the maps, and began to explain the history of the region and America's involvement in it. He had a masterful way of explaining government policies and the unintended consequences that often accompany those policies."

Jill admitted that much of those high school memories had faded, but the recollection of this lesson remained. She described the energy in the classroom created by Mr. Christie's passion for his subject and his desire to capture the hearts and minds of his students. "As a teacher myself, I think about the courage it took to follow the students' interest in this controversial and messy topic. I try to bring that same courage and responsiveness to my classroom."

Here is one thing I know for sure: teaching is much more difficult than it looks. As students or observers, what we see are the actions of a teacher. What we cannot see are the thousands of decisions teachers make in the planning and implementation of a lesson. Mr. Christie must have weighed the options, considered the consequences, and made a choice in the moment. This is what teachers do every minute of every day. Researcher Deborah Lowenberg Ball studies the judgment calls teachers make during the course of a lesson. While observing a teacher, she once counted 20 decisions in the span of 1 minute and 28 seconds, some focusing on instruction and others centering on how to respond to student behavior. Making potentially hundreds of quick (but consequential) decisions during a lesson takes great skill and daring.

I often compare teaching to ice-skating. When I was growing up, ice-skating competitions were frequently aired on television. It always looked so easy, the skaters gliding and twirling across the ice. On a cool December afternoon when I was 10, my mom took us to a temporary rink in Tampa. I put on my rental skates and stepped out onto the ice, my ankles wobbling as I clutched the wall. (In other words, I had zero chance of gliding and twirling.) My mom has a picture from that day, and the panicked expression on my face perfectly captures my experience. It's the same one I see on the faces of new teachers during their first weeks of teaching. Like me, they quickly realize they underestimated the difficulty of the task. Just as no one is born a great ice skater, no one is born a great teacher. Mastery develops with time and practice.

Teachers like Mr. Christie are brave enough to improvise—to abandon their plans. They trust in their ability to make the right decisions and to handle whatever comes up. Responding to a teachable moment or trying a new instructional strategy is always a risk to a teacher's sense of competence. Things can go off the rails quickly in a classroom. Mr. Christie was willing to risk potential rejection of his ideas or lack of understanding from his students. He also risked criticism or disapproval from administrators and parents in order to give students what they needed. He let himself be vulnerable enough to share his views, to talk about a topic so fraught with heartbreak, and to admit that he didn't have all of the answers. In the same way, Mrs. Rivers had the courage to connect with a family in mourning, and Mrs. Downey had the audacity to find a new way to reach resistant boys.

If I began to teach with more courage, would that impact the way my graduate students teach their own students? I thought about the possibilities for my project. By collecting and sharing stories about great teachers, could I magnify their impact? I could already sense how the handful of stories I collected were changing my perspective. I knew I could pull lessons from each one to change the way I teach, parent, and relate to the people in my life. By sharing them, could I help others change for the better? Perhaps the teachers we remember still have much to teach us if we use them as models. I decided it was time to get off the porch and get ready for bed. Tomorrow was the beginning of an adventure, and I needed to be ready.

Applying Lessons on Vulnerability

The stories in this project are inspirational, but they also contain lessons. Nothing has impacted the way I interact with the people I teach, lead, and love more than the lessons on vulnerability. Identifying vulnerability as a theme in the stories led me to reflect on my own willingness to be vulnerable and the impact that was having on my relationships. Showing up with authenticity and openness takes courage, but the rewards are worth the risks. After a deep dive into the literature on this topic, I found ways to apply what I learned. Below are three areas of focus related to vulnerability. Within each area are practices and questions for reflection to help you (and your students) become more courageous and connected.

Area 1: Examining Self-Protection

Think about the situations that move you to armor up in a self-protective stance.

In what ways does this show in your actions or demeanor?

Consider the impact of armoring up on your teaching.

How might a reluctance to be vulnerable and open impact your practice?

Area 2: Building Connections

Connecting with students requires a willingness to be emotionally open and available.

How does your own willingness to be open impact student learning and growth?

Relationships develop over time with evidence of acceptance and trust.

How do you create a classroom culture safe from the risks related to connecting with others?

Area 3: Embracing Uncertainty

Trying something new in the classroom is risky, and new strategies are not likely to be implemented perfectly at first.

What do you tell yourself about your competence as a teacher when trying something new?

Unexpected teaching opportunities can happen in any lesson.

How do you decide when to follow your plan and when to follow the students' lead?

Notes and Works Cited

p. 20   Steele, C. M., & Aronson, J. (1995). Stereotype threat and the intellectual test performance of African Americans. *Journal of Personality and Social Psychology, 69*(5), 797–811.

p. 20   Ayers, W. (2014). *About becoming a teacher.* Teachers College Press.

p. 20   Brown, B. (2012). *Daring greatly : How the courage to be vulnerable transforms the way we live, love, parent, and lead.* Gotham Books.

p. 25   Lowenberg, D. B. (2018). *Just dreams and imperatives: The power of teaching in the struggle for public education.* Annual Presidential Address at the American Educational Research Association. Retrieved from https://www.youtube.com/watch?v=JGzQ7O_SIYY&feature=youtu.be&t=35m26s

3

Lessons on Power

At 6:00 a.m., we pulled out of the driveway and headed the 25 miles to Plant City. I looked at the fields of ripening strawberries stretching along the highway. Brian, juggling a coffee, protein bar, and the steering wheel, eventually broke the silence.

"What are you going to say to get people to stop and talk to you?"

I continued to stare out the window. "I don't know. I guess it will come to me." The truth is, I had considered his question for days but was too anxious to discuss it. Brian always sees himself as a coach, and I wasn't in the mood for advice or a pep talk. As we passed the green fields dotted with red berries, I tried to overcome my fears and negative self-talk. There is no real, imminent danger, I reminded myself. All things considered, this was a low-risk endeavor. But it sure didn't feel that way.

Suddenly, the high school was in sight. It was situated on a quiet road between two pastures of grazing cows. The threat of rain had caused the craft fair to be relocated to a hallway by the gym, so we parked in a side lot and Brian carried the table and two chairs. I brought the sign, a bucket of sand to hold it, and my big, canvas tote. Through the double doors stood Laura and the woman in charge of the event. They got us signed in and ushered us to our spot. Laura is a no-nonsense, take-charge kind of person, and I love that about her. We have developed a pattern over decades: I have crazy ideas, and she makes sure they are realized.

DOI: 10.4324/9781003122029-4

Table and chairs unfolded and sign in bucket, Laura left to help her mom sell wire jewelry and Brian set off in search of more coffee. Before I could object, my twin pillars were gone. Both Brian and Laura are aware of my anxiety, but they never give in to it. I suddenly wished the people in my life were better enablers. I busied myself by rearranging the items on the table, trying out different positions for the pens, notepad, and water bottle, as if it had any bearing on my project. After I'd successfully rearranged everything, I sat down.

The Power of Words

In the space next to me, an older couple and their adult daughter began setting up their wares—wall art and cheese boards made from melted wine bottles. The two women stood back and directed the man as he adjusted the display. Then they left him, off to check out the other vendors. In our adjoining spaces, he sat quietly behind his table, and I sat quietly behind mine. Several minutes later, he looked over at me. "What are you selling?" he asked.

"Oh, I'm not selling anything," I blurted out and then continued on without stopping for a breath. "I'm a professor and I'm collecting stories about the teachers people remember as my research project. I think if we know what makes an impact, we can do more of it. Is there a teacher you remember?" I waited with great anticipation for his response.

"Mrs. Reynolds," he said finally. "She used to smack my hand with a ruler and tell me I would never amount to anything if I didn't pay attention. Boy, I won't ever forget her!" He paused for a minute. "I hated her class, but I worked hard."

This was the moment I had been dreading, though I knew it would eventually come. The memories we carry are tied to strong emotions. Just as some of us hold memories of teachers who helped us develop confidence, many of us also recall teachers who made us feel ashamed of ourselves. Our teachers hold incredible power for healing or harming.

A group of researchers once asked adults about the most overwhelming negative experiences in their lives, and hostile words or behavior from a teacher were mentioned with surprising frequency. They found that boys and children with behavior or attention problems are most at risk for adverse interactions with a teacher. The teacher–student relationship plays a major role in a child's academic, social, and emotional adjustment. And because teachers are the authority, students often blame themselves when conflict arises within that dynamic. Fortunately, the reverse is also true: a teacher's position of authority also intensifies the power of kind words and caring acts.

As I was thinking about how to respond, my craft fair neighbor added to his story.

"You know, years later, when I was working at the grocery store, I used to bag Mrs. Reynolds' groceries," he said. "She lived on the next block, and if she had a lot, I would carry her bags to her house. I remember thinking she was smaller and more frail than she seemed in grade school." He recalled the day Mrs. Reynolds told him that she was hard on the boys for their own good. She explained that discipline was the only way they would get out of the neighborhood and have better lives. "She said she was proud of me," he said. Then he leaned over to shake my hand. "I'm Joe, by the way."

Educational researcher and author Paula Denton studies the impact of teachers' words on how students think, act, and learn. It seems our language doesn't just describe experiences, it shapes experiences. A teacher's choice of words can convey expectations about a student's ability as well as the teacher's own excitement about the subject matter. A teacher's words can influence a student's sense of autonomy, competence, and worth. A teacher's words shape the classroom culture and sense of community. Therefore, words must be carefully and intentionally chosen.

Students rarely tell other adults when they are mistreated by a teacher because it is difficult to talk about experiences that conjure feelings of shame. Shaming can happen in classrooms where teachers believe that toughening up kids will make them more motivated and successful. Shaming can also happen in classrooms where teachers use fear to maintain control. These teachers don't understand that shame is the kryptonite to vulnerability's power. My experience as a researcher leads me to believe there is only a small percentage of teachers who intentionally cause harm, but those few leave a mighty destructive wake.

The Power of Community

As I contemplated notions of power in the classroom, Brian approached with a fresh cup of coffee. "You know, that table is probably a barrier," he suggested. "You might have better luck if you came out from behind it."

A stretch of the legs was welcome, but I was starting to get annoyed with him for always being so direct (and for always being so right). As I moved in front of the table, two women in matching shirts approached. I felt certain Laura had sent them but had no evidence of that. The taller one introduced herself as Lindsey. She told me a bit about their skincare company and the products they were selling. Then Lindsey began to tell me her story.

"My family moved from Virginia to Florida in the middle of my fourth grade year," she said. "I had always been in the same, small school, and was anxious about going to a new one. I suppose I had the same worries all new kids do: What if I get lost? Will anyone sit with me at lunch? Will I be left out at recess? Fortunately, Mrs. Donaldson understood what it was like to be a new kid, and she had a plan."

That first morning, when Lindsey stepped foot into Mrs. Donaldson's classroom, she was seated next to Monica, whom Mrs. Donaldson had chosen to act as Lindsey's guide. Monica would help her follow procedures, navigate the campus, and, most importantly, sit with Lindsey at lunch. "It was as if Mrs. Donaldson anticipated my fears and addressed every one," Lindsey said. Monica took her job very seriously, and thoroughly explained everything. "When it was time for lunch, Monica helped me through the line and even provided a review of the selections on the menu. She introduced me to the other girls at the table and warned me about the mean older kids I should avoid." At recess, Monica made sure Lindsey was included in kickball and showed her where to find the jump ropes.

"I recall Mrs. Donaldson checking on me throughout the day," Lindsey continued. "But she seemed to understand the power of kids teaching kids. Both Monica and I benefited from our relationship. I became more comfortable, and Monica became more confident. Monica and I are still close friends," she said, gesturing to the woman beside her. "Now we run our skincare business together."

I chatted a bit longer with Lindsey and Monica about their memories of fourth grade, considering the ways teachers encourage friendships by creating classrooms where students talk, share, and help each other. Communication is necessary for making social connections, but it is also important for learning. Language is how we process information and understand concepts, but many of us grew up in classrooms with "no talking" rules. Researchers Douglas Fisher, Nancy Frey, and Carol Rothenburg studied the balance of talk in classrooms. They captured a typical exchange, with a teacher asking questions and calling on students to answer, and found that 94% of the words used in the exchange were spoken by the teacher. Both learning and relationships flourish when that balance is shifted. Lindsey, Monica, and I agreed that classrooms (and probably the whole world) would be a better place if kids were allowed to talk more.

With a handful of free skincare samples, I hugged Lindsey and Monica as if I, too, had known them since Mrs. Donaldson's class. I felt awkward standing by the table after my new friends left, but I was determined to collect more stories. I picked up the legal pad and held it like a shield in one hand while I clicked my pen with the other. I took a few steps from the table, hoping to invite a few people over, but they quickly said "No, thank you," and moved past.

I saw Laura coming my way from the other end of the hallway. "I could be wrong, but with that notepad in your hand, people probably assume you're taking a survey or registering voters. I think you'd look more approachable without it." Before

I could respond, she was off again. "I'm going to find the vendor selling strawberry shortcakes," she turned and shouted. "I'll bring you one!"

The Power of Trust

Returning the notepad and pen to the table, I considered what to do with my hands. Crossed arms seemed unapproachable. Hands in the pockets made me look shady. Hands on my hips seemed aggressive. As I struggled to find the right stance, a young woman with bouncing auburn curls approached and grabbed my attention. She smiled and extended her hand.

"Hi, I'm Cindy," she said. "I just saw Laura and she told me to come meet you. We teach together. Honestly, anyone who knew me in high school would be shocked to learn I became a teacher, but I can't imagine doing anything else." Cindy's teenage years had been tumultuous, she admitted, but she credited Mrs. Kinsey, a concerned teacher, with pulling her out of a downward spiral. "I was an intelligent kid, but academics didn't interest me," she said. "I was too busy keeping up with my social scene to keep up with my classwork. There were times when I skipped class to hang out with friends. So, when I was assigned to be Mrs. Kinsey's teaching assistant during sixth period, I was surprised."

On the first day of her new position, Cindy had expected Mrs. Kinsey to deliver a lecture about responsibility and trustworthiness. Instead, she was surprised to find out that Mrs. Kinsey was nonchalant, handing Cindy a stack of papers to alphabetize. After that, a stack of notes and envelopes to deliver to other teachers. "She trusted me to carry out these errands quickly and return to class," Cindy said. "I didn't want to let her down. Eventually, it became more important to impress Mrs. Kinsey than to impress my friends."

She started to stay after school to clean the boards and straighten the room, but in actuality, Cindy just enjoyed talking with Mrs. Kinsey—about music, movies, and other things that interest teenagers. Her teacher would ask about her progress in other classes and offer to help, suggesting Cindy spend more time studying.

"I began to study in her room while she graded and planned. Being Mrs. Kinsey's assistant was a turning point for me," Cindy confided. "When someone you admire believes in you, you work hard to justify that belief."

Cindy and I stood for a bit longer to talk about the power of trust. It seems counterintuitive to extend trust to those who have not proven themselves trustworthy, but Mrs. Kinsey must have realized that feeling trusted can inspire young people to rise. She seemed to understand that the more she trusted Cindy, the more Cindy would try to live up to her expectations. Trust begot trustworthiness. Mrs. Kinsey became a model for Cindy in developing trust with her own students. She explained how she makes personal connections and builds trust intentionally over time.

Decades of research suggests the quality of the student–teacher relationship has an impact on students' academic, social, and emotional outcomes. Strong relationships are grounded in trust. It is a foundational component of any relationship, and it's essential for teaching and learning. Trusting relationships are based on emotional warmth and caring as well as consistent responsiveness from the caregiver. Mrs. Kinsey understood the value of trust. She built it in small ways every day with students like Cindy.

As we finished chatting, Laura returned with two overflowing bowls of legendary Plant City strawberry shortcakes. We said goodbye to Cindy and sat down at the table to eat. "How's the story collecting going?" Laura asked. I tried to describe the feeling of receiving someone's story and the immediate sense of connection.

"It's as if the rest of the crowd disappears, and we both become immersed in the memory," I explained, noting my surprise at the ease and flow of the conversations. Still, I shrugged, "I don't know how to stand or what to say, and my anxiety is surely visible. You have been so kind to send people my way, but you can't always be my recruiter."

Laura smiled at me. "You're just getting started. Relax. You'll find your groove." She got up to throw our empty bowls away and promised she'd check back with me later. I hoped she was right. I couldn't see how this process would ever feel comfortable. I had no trouble staying engaged in the conversations—that part did feel easy and natural—but soliciting participants was difficult for me. If only people would just notice the sign and approach me.

The Power of Love

By 1:00 p.m. I was running out of energy and had reclaimed one of the chairs behind the table. I looked up to see a man approaching slowly with a limp. He looked from me to the empty chair at my right. I waved my hand inviting him to join me, and he gladly accepted. "Hello there," he said as he took a seat. "I'm John." He lowered himself slowly, apologizing for his bad knee. I noticed his crisp linen shirt and perfectly creased jeans as he sat. I told him about my project and asked if he remembered a special teacher. He smiled as he recalled Miss Andrews, his third grade teacher.

"We were as poor as a family could be without living on the streets," John began. "I don't think I was aware of that until I went to school. I remember seeing other kids in their clean, pressed clothes and thinking they must be loved in a way that I longed to be. My dad was too busy drinking, and my mom was too busy getting beaten by my dad to take care of me. I started to press my own clothes, but they never looked as new and clean as the clothes of the kids I admired." Miss Andrews, John remembered, would invite him to her home after school for a snack, recognizing that he was often hungry.

One day as he was leaving, she handed him a package wrapped in brown paper and tied with string. John ran all the way home, anxious to open it. "I spent hours staring at the three new school shirts that had been folded inside the package, holding them and smelling them," John said. "It still gets to me.

You are supposed to love your own children, but this woman showed such love to someone else's child. Looking back, I know she couldn't have had much herself, and yet, she made this sacrifice for me. Somebody noticed me. Somebody cared about me."

We both sat there in silence for a moment. Then John continued, explaining why he remembered this moment so clearly and why it continued to affect him so profoundly. Reflecting back on his childhood, John realized that he could have taken two different paths: become an addict and abuser like his father or make something of himself. It was Miss Andrews who helped him realize he was worthy of health and happiness, and by instilling a sense of worth, she helped change the trajectory of his life. John became a firefighter and saved the lives of countless people. He became a father and showed his two daughters the love he wished he had been given.

Psychologist Julius Segal studied at-risk youth, those who are less likely to transition successfully into adulthood. With a myriad of factors working against them, such as poverty and abuse, some children developed resilience and succeeded, while others struggled. One factor that helped them beat the odds was a caring adult who took an interest in their lives and helped them gather strength. In many cases, this was a teacher. It's easy to assume that momentous events change lives, but lives are often changed in small moments. By noticing John's needs and responding, Miss Andrews became a critical figure in his path to a better life, and her gift—a perfectly packaged stack of new shirts—sent him a clear message: You are seen. You are loved. John's story exemplifies the power of simple acts and the meaning children take from them.

As I sat there pondering the impact of teachers like Miss Andrews, an announcement was made that the craft fair was ending. Brian, who'd spent the afternoon just out of sight, returned to pack up the table and chairs while I carefully slid my notes and consent forms into my tote bag. Laura stopped by to help and we agreed to debrief on the phone later. I was tired, but there was a sense of satisfaction in getting the project off the ground. I am always amazed when a plan comes together.

The Power of Passion

On the way home, I thought about Joe, Lindsey, Monica, Cindy, and John, people who had been strangers just a few hours ago but who now seemed more like friends. We drove past the strawberry fields in silence until Brian's words interrupted my thoughts.

"How did it go?"

"I think there's something interesting here," I answered. "The stories I collected today are inherently beautiful, but I also think they could be useful models for teachers, or for anyone who wants to make a difference." I relayed Joe's story to Brian, along with my realization that it would not be the last discouraging memory I would collect. I told him about Lindsey and Monica and the delightful classroom culture their teacher created, and Cindy and John, who both experienced a transformation under the care of dedicated teachers. I talked about my own excitement for the project and my doubts about my ability to do it justice. With eyes on the road, Brian just listened, nodded, and smiled.

The drive home that day was a turning point in my journey: I was certain that if I continued, I would find many more stories and memories that had the potential to teach us all how to make a bigger impact on the lives of those around us. If I kept going, I could provide a way for memorable teachers to continue making an impact, even those who are no longer with us. I knew this passion would carry me. I just needed to figure out where to go next.

Applying Lessons on Power

Being mindful of the power inherent in my profession has made me more intentional about the words I use and more conscious of the meaning students may infer from my actions. Identifying power as a theme in the stories also led me to reflect on my own experiences as a student, particularly my experiences in classrooms where teachers used fear and shame as tools for classroom management. Using the power of love and connection takes more time and energy, but the reward is worth the effort. After delving into the literature on this topic, I found ways to apply what I had learned. Below are three areas of focus related to power. Within each area are practices and questions for reflection to help you better understand the power that your words and actions have in shaping your students' lives.

Area 1: Examining the Power of Your Words

Record yourself interacting with students for brief periods over a few days.

What messages do your words and tone convey?

Note some words and phrases you would like to use more often and keep them where you can see them.

What would you intentionally like to convey to students about their competence and worth?

Area 2: The Power of Community

Use your recordings to note the balance of teacher talk vs. student talk in the classroom.

How can you give students more time to talk with each other?

Observe your students in the lunchroom or in social situations.

Who is connected? Who is often alone? How can you facilitate connections among your students?

Area 3: Hidden Messages

Consider how students are receiving messages about their own worth.

What are these messages? Where are the messages originating?

Consider the messages you send through small acts of care and kindness.

How can you help students feel more important and worthy?

Notes and Works Cited

p. 31   Brengden, M., Wanner, B., Vitaro, F. (2006). Verbal abuse by the teacher and child adjustment from kindergarten through grade 6. *Pediatrics 177*(5), 1585–1609.

p. 31   Denton, P. (2007). *The power of our words : Teacher language that helps children learn*. Northeast Foundation for Children, Inc.

p. 33   Fisher, D., Frey, N., Rothenburg, C. (2008). *Content-area conversations: How to plan discussion based lessons for diverse language learners*. ASCD.

p. 35   Russell, S., Wentzel, K., Donlan, A. (2016). Teachers' beliefs about the development of teacher-adolescent trust. *Learning Environment Research. 19*:241–246.

p. 37   Segal, J. (1988). Teachers have enormous power in affecting a child's self-esteem. *The Brown University Child Behavior and Development Newsletter. 4*:1–3.

4

Lessons on Connection

One of my favorite spots to work is the second floor of Roux Library on the western edge of campus. In addition to rows and rows of books, there's a big picture window with a view of Lake Hollingsworth in the distance. Most importantly, there are long tables, big enough to allow me to spread out all of the quotes and notes I had gathered so far. My purpose for this project was to identify the ways teachers (like my Mrs. Russell) made a lasting impact on their students' lives. I had accumulated over 50 stories at this point—enough to begin analyzing the data. I emptied my tote bag of all of the papers, packs of colored highlighters, and a big bottle of aspirin (data analysis is not for the weak).

I was using the Grounded Theory approach, originally developed by Barney Glaser and Anslem Strauss. This approach requires simultaneously collecting, coding, and analyzing data in an ongoing, circular process. I began coding the stories and notes that covered the table by looking for common words and phrases, and found myself highlighting the words *trust*, *caring*, *patient*, *kind*, *nurturing*. Once I had identified these common concepts, I thought about the deeper meaning. That's where it got messy. I made a list of inferences and tried out a few ideas to see how they fit. I eliminated some and expanded on others, all while making copious notes in my journal, stopping just long enough to pop an aspirin and chase it down with a swig of cold coffee.

DOI: 10.4324/9781003122029-5

Feeling Safe

Alex, a student worker in the library, approached just as I needed a break. He had come up to the second floor to shelve some books. Alex was accustomed to my chaotic tablescapes and always expressed interest in my projects. He peered over my shoulder. "Whatcha working on, Dr. H?"

I put down my pen. "I'm trying to understand what teachers say and do that makes a difference in their students' lives."

Alex listened as I told him about the way Mrs. Donaldson alleviated Lindsey's fears, the way Mrs. Kinsey built trust with Cindy, and the way Miss Andrews cared for John.

"That's beautiful," Alex responded. "It's like these teachers saw their students' fears and uncertainties, and they created a safe space for them."

Alex went back to shelving books, and I considered his words. The notion of feeling safe seemed to encapsulate the words and phrases I had highlighted. That was it. Students remember teachers who make them feel safe, who take away their need for self-protection, who allow them to take the risks necessary for learning and growth. I wrote the word *safe* in my journal and checked again to see how this interpretation fit with the data.

Alex finished one row and came back by the table. "Now you've made me think about the teachers I remember. I had so many great teachers."

I asked him to tell me about one of them, and Alex shared a story about Miss Davis, his fourth grade teacher.

"I was nine when my mom went back to work," he began. "It was a big change for me because I was used to having her around to fix me breakfast, take me to school, and drop things off that I forgot." Alex explained that when his mom started working she left the house before he did, so he had to ride his bike to school. "I tried to be tough and pretend I was fine," he admitted, "but the truth is, I felt anxious and alone. Miss Davis seemed to understand that I was having a hard time, and she greeted me at the classroom door every morning when I arrived."

Alex leaned on the book cart. "One January morning, I started my bike ride and realized halfway to school that I had forgotten my gloves." He noted that he lived in Florida and his school was only a few blocks away, but in Alex's young mind, it was well below freezing and miles away. "Somewhere along the ride, I started to cry. I finally made it to my classroom, shivering, with tears running down my cheeks. Miss Davis bent down, and without saying a word, she held my hands in hers and rubbed them until they were warm."

I shook my head in wonder. "I'm amazed that you remember that small moment from so long ago."

"Miss Davis was always doing things like that. She would notice when something was wrong and try to make it better. She did these little things with a big, open heart. For some reason, that January morning sticks in my memory."

Alex and I both proclaimed the significance of small acts of kindness. We were in awe of teachers, like Miss Davis, who consistently notice and respond to students' needs.

Beyond Transactional

As Alex returned to the stacks, I turned back to my notes and considered his story as it related to the notion of safety. Feeling safe was certainly part of teacher impact, but there was more to it. Analysis is an ongoing process, and I needed to collect more data to get a more complete picture. When I finally pulled myself out of my thoughts and looked at the time, I realized I was running late. I quickly packed up my tote bag and hustled out of the library toward the education building, where students were likely waiting for our weekly dissertation writers support meeting.

When I entered the room, Kat, Chris, and Rafael were already updating each other about their progress. When they finished, they turned to me. I appreciated being held equally accountable by these future colleagues and worked my way back into their good graces by explaining my tardiness. I told them about my analysis so far and then shared Alex's story. "I'm mystified that someone would carry such a detailed memory for over a decade," I said. "I keep wondering why students remember some school experiences so clearly but not others." They paused as they considered my query.

Kat spoke first. "I do recall specific teachers and classrooms, and not because of any big event or dramatic experience. I think mostly it's the way I felt," she said. "It's like my memories of those teachers and classrooms are clear and in color while much of the rest of my memories are in kind of a grayscale blur."

Rafael nodded. "When I think about those fuzzy memories, it seems those classrooms were mostly transactional. The teacher assigned the work, I did the work, the teacher graded the work. It's like we fulfilled an agreement so that we could get through it. Most of those teachers were kind enough, but we were all just going through the motions," he said. "The clear memories come from classrooms where I felt a connection, where the teacher and I related as humans. We were engaged with the content, or at the very least, engaged with each other."

We all sat for a few minutes considering our discussion, and then the three emerging scholars opened their laptops and attended to their own research. After our session, I walked back to my office thinking about the notion of transactional teaching versus responsive teaching. Responsive teaching prioritizes the needs of the student over curriculum or instructional strategies. Social psychologist Harry Reis suggests relationships with students are stronger when students perceive their teacher is responsive and demonstrates understanding, validation, and caring. According to Dr. Reis, understanding is often perceived as, *My teacher knows who I am and what's important to me.* Students perceive validation as, *My teacher respects who I am and what I want.* Caring is commonly perceived as, *My teacher takes active and supportive steps to help me meet my needs.* When a student feels known, valued, and cared for, that student is more likely to characterize the relationship with a teacher in terms of comfort and warmth. And that teacher is more likely to be remembered as having a positive impact on the student's life.

Bids for Connection

How do teachers demonstrate responsiveness and build relationships in the classroom? Researcher and author John Gottman suggests that it starts with bids for connection. Bids are attempts to get attention, affirmation, affection, or any other positive connection. They can be subtle (like a gesture or facial expression) or overt (like a question or request for help). There are three ways to respond to bids: turning toward, turning against, or turning away. To turn toward means to respond in a positive, affirming way, while turning against may look like belittling, being argumentative, or being aggressive. Turning against obviously damages relationships, but so does turning away, which involves ignoring a bid. Turning away may be done intentionally, but more often, it happens because we are preoccupied.

Recently, while visiting a friend's classroom, I witnessed the power of responding to bids for connection. Amanda (a high school English teacher) and I were working on a project together. We met during her sixth period planning time, and she invited me to stay through her seventh period class so that we could finish our work after school. Taking a seat in the back, I watched as the students entered the classroom. I noticed one trudge in with his sweatshirt hood over his head and a scowl on his face. He dropped his backpack with a loud thump and slumped down into his seat, arms crossed. Amanda walked over to her desk, scribbled something on a notepad, and nonchalantly slid the note to the student. A few minutes after reading the note, the student pushed the hood off his head and his shoulders relaxed. Just before class started, he pulled out his book and began to read.

I could hardly wait until the students left to find out what Amanda had written. It turns out that the note simply said, "Looks like you're having a tough day. I'm glad you're here. Let me know if I can help." Recognizing and turning toward her student's bid took only a moment of Amanda's time, but it clearly made a difference in his day. I wondered what may have happened if she had responded by turning against it. She might have said, "You need to take that hood off. Don't come in here with that attitude." It could have escalated an already frustrated young man. What if she had turned away, just ignored the bid? He may not have disturbed others, but he probably would not have been engaged in learning.

Bids for connection happen in classrooms all day, every day, and strong relationships are characterized by turning toward those bids as often as possible. It occurred to me that making a difference in students' lives wasn't just about helping them feel safe. It was also about making them feel seen. It was about demonstrating through actions that students are worthy of their teacher's time and attention.

I knew I needed to collect more data to dive deeper into the concepts of safe and seen and to get a more comprehensive understanding of teacher impact. I was ready to try story-collecting at a bigger, busier venue, someplace that would attract a variety of people. I had the perfect spot in mind: a booth at the Lakeland Downtown Farmers' Market. The Farmers' Market is one of my favorite weekend happenings, so it felt comfortable and familiar. A little online searching revealed a small number of booths available for non-profit use. I decided that this applied to educational researchers, and headed downtown to secure a spot.

Feeling Stretched

After submitting my application for a booth, I stopped into Mitchell's coffee shop for a piece of their famous Coca-Cola cake. Perched on a stool by the window, I scanned the notes in my research journal and wondered what was missing in my analysis so far. What else was there beyond the concepts of safe and seen?

I was so deep in thought that I hardly noticed a tall woman sit down next to me. She pointed at her own cake. "Isn't this the best? I just can't help myself." Then she glanced at my notebook. "Are you a writer?"

I briefly explained my role and my current research project. After a bite of cake, she confessed, "My name is Cathy. I'm the oldest of three kids raised by a single mom. When I started school, I realized that my mom couldn't do all of the things some of the other moms did. She couldn't volunteer in our class or help me with projects. I knew my mom loved me, but I always wanted more of her attention."

I wasn't sure where Cathy was going with this, but then she began to talk about her kindergarten teacher, Mrs. Nash. "I remember feeling envious of my classmates who could tie their own shoes. In January, each student chose a goal to post on a New Year bulletin board. Mine was simple—learn to tie my shoelaces." Cathy went on to explain that not long after her goal was posted, Mrs. Nash called her mom to ask if she could keep Cathy after school for a few days and then walk her to daycare. "During those after school sessions, my teacher sat next to me on the floor, patiently showing me how to make two bunny ears out of my laces, crisscross the tree, jump into the hole and pop out the other side. It took several tries, but I soon became an expert at tying laces."

Then Cathy said something every teacher needs to hear. "I felt so proud and so independent, and the time Mrs. Nash spent teaching me made me feel special. I knew my teacher was busy. She probably had at least fifteen other students to care for each day, but she took that time to focus on just me." We talked for a few more minutes about the small things that make a big impact on kids. Then my fellow cake-lover boxed up the rest of her slice and headed off to the gym.

I returned to my journal, thinking about how Cathy's story related to the concepts of safe and seen. Mrs. Nash turned toward Cathy's bid for connection, and in doing so, satisfied her need for attention and helped her reach a goal. In this case, the turning toward communicated value to Cathy, and it surely deepened the relationship with her teacher.

Educational researcher Robert Pianta has spent decades studying student–teacher relationships as a lever to improve academic, social, and emotional outcomes for students. According to Dr. Pianta, the type and quality of a teacher's interactions with a student impacts the student's ability to demonstrate social competence with peers, self-regulate emotions, and persist at academic tasks. Teachers' interactions fall into three categories. The first category involves emotional support—interactions that foster a sense of connection and caring. The next category includes interactions that promote classroom organization, like setting routines or managing behavior. The third involves instructional support—interactions that encourage academic achievement and cognitive press.

I was feeling challenged to fit the third category, instructional support, into the concepts of safe and seen. Emotionally supportive interactions would elicit feeling safe. And Dr. Pianta's research suggested the importance of teacher sensitivity, characterized by a timely response that shows awareness of the student's perspective. This sensitivity would engender feeling seen. But instructionally supportive interactions were more about feeling stretched. These interactions focus on stretching a student's thinking or understanding. Not in a transactional way, as in just presenting the concepts or assigning discrete learning tasks (as Rafael had described), but in a deeper, more responsive way. Stretched seemed to be the missing component. I began to consider how memorable teachers helped students feel safe, seen, and stretched in the classroom.

Visualizing Potential

It was late in the evening when I finally settled into the den and opened my laptop. Several heated school board races were happening in our county, and I was closely following Anita Carson's campaign. Anita is a middle school teacher, and she is passionate about improving the working conditions for teachers in the district. I joined her virtual event already in progress and listened to her plans. When I heard her talk about her inspiration, her third grade teacher, I made a note to reach out to her.

Despite her jam-packed calendar, Anita found a few minutes to chat with me. After a brief discussion about her campaign, I asked her to tell me about Mrs. Herron. "In third grade, I struggled with reading," she began. "The letters always seemed jumbled up on the page. I now know it was dyslexia, but so little was understood about it back then." Anita told me Mrs. Herron was the first to realize what was causing her struggle, and she tried several interventions to see what might help. "She cut letters out of sandpaper and glued them to construction paper so I could practice feeling what a letter should 'look like.' When I started interacting with the letters kinesthetically instead of just visually, things began to click."

Anita eventually experienced success. "By the end of third grade, I could even read and write complex patterns, like 'ough.'" Her success with the sandpaper letters led to her finding other ways to compensate. "School stopped being so frustrating. I felt like Mrs. Herron saw me as a whole person, with strengths and potential, and not just a kid with low reading scores. Now that I'm a teacher, I try to see each of my students as a human first, rather than a test score or a data point. I take the time to figure out what works for each one like Mrs. Herron did for me."

My conversation with Anita added another dimension to the concepts of safe, seen, and stretched. Mrs. Herron didn't just see Anita as she was, she also saw what Anita could be. She saw potential. She saw a reader. Mrs. Herron had a vision of Anita's success, and she committed to realizing that vision. It's not difficult to believe in the potential of students who demonstrate academic proficiency, but teachers like Mrs. Herron believe in the potential of all students. Unfortunately, many teachers proclaim that all students can succeed but, deep down, don't really believe it. What has become known as the "belief gap" in education often results from hidden biases related to a student's race, ethnicity, gender, or label. Equity of opportunities for all students depends on holding equally high expectations for all students. Closing the belief gap requires reflection and effort, but the payoff is worth the effort, especially for students like Anita.

Dr. Pianta's research on student–teacher relationships suggests that improving relationships can lead to greater academic success for students with academic risk factors, like Anita. Dr. Pianta also found supportive relationships with teachers to be a protective factor for children with risks, such as economic instability. Children from economically stable homes with a college-educated parent tend to arrive at kindergarten more prepared for academics than peers without these advantages.

Too often, this achievement gap increases as students progress through school. However, when teachers consistently provide emotional and instructional support through their interactions with students, those with non-academic risk factors tend to make gains at the same rate as their peers. The impact of effective and supportive teachers over consecutive years can greatly reduce differences in achievement. Mrs. Herron was the start of a positive trajectory in Anita's academic journey.

Relationships as Intervention

Certainly, students must be active participants in pursuit of their own learning. How do we motivate students to be academically engaged? Educational researchers Tricia Valeski and Deborah Stipek found that students' feelings about school and feelings about themselves as learners have implications for academic engagement and success. They identified relationships with teachers as a contributing factor to students' feelings about school, and therefore, a positive influence on academic achievement.

Strong student–teacher relationships also inspire student collaboration in maintaining a safe and positive learning environment. Often, what is characterized as misbehavior is really a conflict between a student and a teacher. Creating a classroom where students feel safe and seen, where there is greater comfort and less conflict, can prevent or reduce behavior problems. Creating a classroom where students feel stretched, where they feel supported and challenged, can increase engagement. In classrooms where students feel safe, seen, and stretched, they cooperate because they are valued members of a community, not to avoid punishment or gain reward. Imagine, then, the power of intentionally focusing on student–teacher relationships as part of a student's academic or disciplinary intervention plan.

I finally closed my laptop and my journal. Tomorrow was going to be a busy day, and we still needed to pack up the car. I was anxious about collecting stories at the farmers' market but eager to see how this additional data would fit into the concepts of safe, seen, and stretched.

Applying Lessons on Connection

Since encountering the research on building strong relationships I've become more intentional in my interactions. Consistently turning toward bids for connection has required me to focus my attention on those in front of me, rather than attending to my mental to-do list or the chatter in my own head. I can see the positive impact of my efforts on my students, but I did not anticipate the satisfaction and joy these practices would bring me in return. Below are three areas of focus for greater connection.

Area 1: Noticing and Responding to Bids for Connection

Consider the experience each student is having in your classroom and see if you can recognize bids for connection. Find simple ways to turn toward bids as often as possible. When you're not able to respond immediately, quickly give an assurance that you noticed and will respond when you can.

How does your effort to respond to students' bids influence your classroom environment?

How does your effort to respond to students' bids contribute to your own feelings of satisfaction and joy in teaching?

Area 2: Interacting in Supportive Ways

Record yourself interacting with students (or review the interactions you previously recorded).

Do your responses show an awareness of the students' perspectives?

How often do your responses provide emotional or instructional support?

How timely are your responses to students' needs?

Area 3: Strengthening Relationships as Interventions

Choose one student who challenges you (because of academic or behavioral needs).

Make an effort to notice and respond to the student's bids for connection as often as possible.

What happens when you make an effort to meet the needs of this student?

What happens when you make an effort to help this student feel understood and validated?

What else might help this student feel more connected with you and with classmates?

Notes and Works Cited

p. 41   Glasser, B. & Strauss, A. (1967). *The discovery of grounded theory.* Adeline.

p. 44   Reis, H. T., Lemay, E. P., Jr., & Finkenauer, C. (2017). Toward understanding understanding: The importance of feeling understood in relationships. *Social and Personality Psychology Compass, 11*(3).

p. 45   Gottman, J. M. and DeClaire, J. (2001). *The relationship cure: A five step guide to strengthening your marriage, family, and friendships.* Crown Publishers.

p. 47   Pianta, R. C. (1999). *Enhancing relationships between children and teachers.* American Psychological Association.

p. 49   Pianta, R. C., & Walsh, D. J. (1996). *High-risk children in schools : constructing sustaining relationships.* Routledge.

p. 50   Valeski, T.N. and Stipek, D.J. (2001), Young children's feelings about school. Child Development. 72, 1198–1213.

5

Lessons on Expectations

We pulled up to the corner of Kentucky Avenue and Pine Street to find Jim, the manager of the Lakeland Downtown Farmers' Market, who directed us to space 42. The 10-foot by 10-foot square was marked in chalk on the brick road, ready to be filled with our folding table, chairs, and the pop-up tent we borrowed from our friend, Jack. The two Professors Hasson (not known for our engineering skills) managed to assemble the tent, add sandbags to the poles for stability, and arrange the furniture underneath. I added a big potted fern we brought along to hold my sign.

The market was buzzing in the early morning light, with vendors setting up for blocks on either side of our space. Sweet smells were drifting over from the bakery booth, and cheerful tones vibrated from the steel drum artists down the street. With little chance of rain and a soft morning breeze, it was shaping up to be a perfect day at the market, and I was hopeful that the pleasant conditions would inspire people to slow down and chat. As the first few patrons came north on Kentucky, I stationed myself by the sign and tried to look welcoming.

Seeds of Hope

One woman in gray running tights and a tank top slowed down long enough to read the sign. She glanced over at me and shouted, "My fourth grade teacher—she made my life hell!"

DOI: 10.4324/9781003122029-6

Before I could respond, she put her headphones in and continued down the road. A bit shell shocked, I glanced over at Brian who was standing in the back of the tent.

He looked amused. "Well, that's some data for you," he said, making his way across the street. "I'm heading to Mitchell's for some coffee. Get back out there. The day has just begun."

That first encounter had deflated me a bit, not just because of the aggressive way she responded, but also because I wished I could have heard the reasoning behind her words. We can learn just as much from the painful memories as the joyful ones. Luckily, another woman was approaching. I lifted my shoulders up, trying to appear confident and friendly. Even though she was carrying bags of tomatoes, cucumbers, and green beans, she stopped to talk with me.

"My name is Lisa," she began, "and I would love to tell you about Mrs. Grisham, my second grade teacher." Lisa described the small, rural town where she was raised. There were several family farms, and most of the town's residents were just getting by on the money they made from farming. She explained that most young people would stay and work on the farms and that it was difficult for them to imagine any other options. Lisa shifted her bags from one arm to the other. "During the first week of second grade," she said, "Mrs. Grisham asked us to write about what we wanted to be when we grew up. A few of us really wanted to be farmers, but the rest of us had different dreams. Mrs. Grisham began to call us by the titles of the professions to which we aspired. I became Lisa the teacher. Some of my classmates were Amy the nurse, Tom the banker and Bill the scientist. Our teacher was one of the few people who talked about the possibilities for our lives and helped us visualize our futures."

Twenty years later, Lisa said, she went back to visit her former teacher. "I wanted her to know I became a teacher, just as she predicted. I wanted to thank her for helping me believe it could happen. During my visit, Mrs. Grisham explained that she grew up the daughter of a farmer. She went off to college and came back to make a difference. I told her that she will always be my model for growing hope in the hearts and minds of my own students."

As Lisa walked away, I realized that my mood had shifted. I didn't have to try to lift my shoulders anymore and my sense of optimism returned. Just hearing Lisa's story filled me with joy and with gratitude for teachers like Mrs. Grisham. In some ways, I thought to myself, Lisa's teacher did become a farmer, planting seeds of hope in her students. Mrs. Grisham may not always get to see what grows from those seeds, but every once in a while, a student reaches out to show her.

Self-Fulfilling Prophecies

With a bit of a lull in the crowd, I paused to think about Lisa's story and the power of expectations. Early evidence that teacher expectations impact student outcomes came from a partnership between psychologist Robert Rosenthal and principal Lenore Jacobson. In 1965 the pair conducted an experiment, telling teachers that certain students could be expected to make unusually sizable gains in growth based on the students' results on the Harvard Test of Inflected Acquisition. In fact, the identified students had been randomly chosen and the test did not exist. For the first and second graders in the study, the teachers' beliefs resulted in gains far greater than those in the control group. This phenomenon became known as The Pygmalion Effect, and it has been replicated in multiple studies over the decades since Rosenthal and Jacobson's original study.

Dr. Rosenthal suggests that teacher expectations have a self-fulfilling prophecy effect in that, when teachers hold high expectations for student success, they interact with students in ways that affirm their expectations. It's not the teachers' beliefs themselves that facilitate student growth, it's the actions that stem from those beliefs. Our beliefs about our students influence our actions toward them and our interactions with them. These actions and interactions then influence the beliefs students cultivate about themselves. And students' self-beliefs motivate them to act in ways that lead to their own growth. The words we speak and the actions we take (or don't take) have an undeniable impact on our students' lives. Mrs. Grisham understood that and intentionally communicated high expectations. She believed in her students so they could believe in themselves.

The Power of Placement

I was pulled back into the present moment by a man with a young girl on his shoulders. She had one arm wrapped around his head and was holding a cookie in the other hand. He turned toward me. "Either you're not selling anything or you've had an exceptionally good morning and already sold out." I laughed and briefly explained my project. He responded, "That's cool! I'm Emilio and this is Emily."

I looked up. "Hi, Emily! Do you go to school?" I asked. "Can you tell me about your teacher?" She put her head down and tried to hide behind her dad.

"She's being shy," Emilio said. "But I can tell you about my favorite teacher, Mrs. Rubens."

Emilio remembered his neighborhood as a place where kids dreamed about being athletes or recording artists, but nobody planned on going to college. He said, "Being a good student wasn't cool, and we went to school to socialize. I got in trouble a lot, and I didn't apply myself. I was bored most of the time, and I just didn't see the point."

He described Mrs. Rubens' language arts class as the one class he didn't hate in eighth grade. In that class, he read books he liked, and Mrs. Rubens got the students to talk about the books. "The problem was," Emilio explained, "some kids in there gave me a hard time, and I felt like I had to show them I wasn't into reading. I felt bad about disrupting Mrs. Rubens' class."

Emilio put Emily down. "Mrs. Rubens made me stay after class one day and told me I was getting a schedule change. She asked the principal to place me in her advanced class. She said I was smart. She said I was capable. I told her I didn't want to move classes, but she said the decision was already made." Emilio admitted feeling out of place in the advanced class at first. "These kids weren't playing. They wanted to learn. They were going places. But they were nice to me, and they asked me what

I thought about the things we read. They worked with me on projects. I started to see myself as one of the smart kids."

Emilio called it a turning point in his life. He told me it was the point when he realized he had options. If he worked hard, he could have a better future. And, Emilio added, "I invited Mrs. Rubens to my college graduation."

As I was waving goodbye to Emilio and Emily, Brian returned with a tea for me. I shared Lisa's story and Emilio's story, and he affirmed what I was thinking. "When you're a kid, there's something really compelling about an adult, someone in a position of authority, believing in your ability." The stories, and Brian's comment, had me thinking about how students come to understand what their teachers believe about them.

Differentiation vs. Determination

Rhona Weinstein, a psychologist and educational researcher, has spent decades learning from children about their teachers' expectations for them and their peers. According to Dr. Weinstein, students perceive that their teachers treat those who perform well differently from those who struggle. Most of the clues that students use to identify their relative ability in the classroom come from the words or actions of their teachers, not their own appraisals or the opinions of their parents. Because teachers make the decisions and drive the actions in the classroom, children see teachers as the arbiters of what smartness is and who has it.

Comparisons may happen openly in classrooms, such as scores on a chart or comments in front of the class. More often, however, comparisons of ability in classrooms are more subtle. Students intuitively compare a teacher's interactions with peers to the teacher's interactions with themselves. What instructional behaviors give students these clues? Placement in leveled groups is one way that students rank performance in classrooms. When they are grouped by ability, they naturally try to understand the hierarchy. Even young children are quickly able to identify the high-performing group. Students also infer expectations from the way teachers ask questions, both in who they call on to answer and how they respond to answers.

I observed this in a recent visit to an elementary school. The principal was concerned that some students were not making learning gains and invited me to spend a few days observing and interviewing students. I came into a third grade classroom just as the teacher was beginning a science lesson. She asked a terrific higher order question, one that required the students to think. Then she pulled a random popsicle stick to call on a student to respond. The small, redheaded boy whose name was on the stick squirmed in his seat. The teacher quickly asked, "Do you want to phone a friend?" He then called the name of another boy who provided the answer. The teacher praised the correct answer, and continued with the lesson. Then for independent practice, she distributed a diagram for students to label.

When the students started working, I pulled my chair up next to the boy she had called on. I asked him to tell me about phoning a friend. His response was revealing. "She doesn't let the smart kids phone a friend," he said. "Only us kids who don't do well get to." I was struck by his honesty, and I stuck around for the next lesson. I realized he was right. With some students, the teacher restated the question, probed, and scaffolded until they figured out the answer. With other students, she quickly offered the phone-a-friend escape. I believe she had the best of intentions, but her actions were sending a powerful message.

It's not just questioning and grouping that give students clues about expectations; they also make inferences based on the tasks teachers assign. When students who are identified as high-achieving are given choice in their assignments while students who struggle are given rote tasks, the difference in assignments leads to inferences about differences in ability. Teachers often feel the need for tighter control over the curriculum with students who struggle. They assume gaps in performance are due to a lack of motivation. But the restriction of choice and voice may, in itself, be a contributing factor in motivation. The amount and type of feedback given to different students also leads to inferences about their teachers' expectations.

When students perceive their teachers are giving discretionary effort and making an investment in their success, they come to believe they must be worthy of that effort and investment. They make inferences about their own potential. On the flip side, a lack of interaction, simply assigning tasks with little regard for students' needs or interest, and giving minimal feedback send strong messages about a students' lack of potential. What Rafael, my doctoral student, described as transactional is exactly the type of teaching that communicates low expectations. Communicating high expectations is an essential action in helping students feel safe, seen, and stretched.

Consistency and Conviction

Back at the farmers' market, I was jotting notes about expectations in my journal and sipping some tea when I noticed a tall young man with an engaging smile heading my way. He asked a few questions about my project and then identified himself as Jay, a teacher at the high school down the street. "I'm realizing that many of us became educators because we were inspired by a teacher," I said to him, shaking his hand. "Was there a particular teacher who influenced you to go into education?"

Jay responded without hesitation. "Mr. Mann is the reason I got through the required math classes to graduate from high school and then went on to graduate from college." Jay explained that by the time he started in Mr. Mann's class, he had already failed algebra once. "I was a confident kid in high school, but math intimidated me. Walking into Mr. Mann's class that first day, I had little hope of success."

Jay still remembered his teacher's words from that first day of class. Mr. Mann told his students they would have a quiz at the start of each class. The quiz would only cover what they did the previous day. All they had to do was show up every day, pay attention, and go over the material when they got home.

Jay recalled being aware of the high stakes, and he did precisely what Mr. Mann said. He came to class every day, took notes, and reviewed his notes every evening. "It seemed less overwhelming to just focus on one day's lesson at a time," Jay said. "As days turned into weeks, I began to master the content.

Halfway through the semester, I was helping other students. I did not just pass algebra; I made the highest grade in the class."

That experience with Mr. Mann continues to influence his life, Jay said. "Now, whenever I am faced with a difficult task, I think about Mr. Mann. I know anything is doable if I just break it down into bite-sized chunks." And he recognizes Mr. Mann's influence on his own teaching. "Whether I'm working with the students in my classroom or the players on my basketball team, I communicate an unwavering belief in their ability to succeed. Then I provide the tools and structure they need to achieve their goals."

Confidence and Competence

As Jay walked away, I thought about the difference between the terms "low-performing" and "under-performing." Calling students low-performing infers a limit on their capability. It suggests students are performing to the best of their limited ability. Under-performing, however, suggests students are not yet performing to their potential. The truth is, as educators, we have no way of knowing a student's potential. Past performance is not necessarily a predictor of future performance. According to Yvette Jackson, the Chief Executive Officer of the National Urban Alliance for Effective Education, under-performing students have often received under-challenging instruction.

According to Dr. Jackson, teachers can build the competence and confidence of all students by creating bridges between their students' cultural experiences and the content. Teachers can teach for understanding by helping students construct meaning, and teachers can assess that understanding by designing performance tasks that acknowledge cultural differences. Competence in a subject is language dependent. Students must acquire the language and vocabulary of the subject or discipline, be able to construct meaning from discipline-specific texts, and be able to communicate that meaning. Lacking language proficiency is not necessarily an indicator of lack of ability. On the contrary, it is often an indicator of lack of effective instruction.

I kept mulling over Jay's story, imagining the outcome if he had not encountered Mr. Mann, if his last experience in an advanced math class ended in failure. It was Mr. Mann's instruction, and the structure he provided, not Jay's ability, that made the difference. As Jay grew in competence, he grew in confidence. Although it seems Mr. Mann was not one for passionate, motivational speeches, his quiet yet unwavering belief was evident to Jay.

I stayed at my post through lunch, and my persistence paid off with six more stories. It was a lovely (and productive) day at the farmers' market. I had more data to hold up against the concepts of safe, seen, and stretched. I had a deeper understanding of the power of expectations. I knew this would not be my last data collection day on the warm, brick streets of downtown Lakeland. But for now, my head was full and my feet were tired. We packed up the contents of space 42 and headed back home.

Applying Lessons on Expectations

The idea of communicating high expectations for all students has been around for decades. The challenge lies in the subtle ways high expectations are communicated. Students make inferences about our expectations based on our instructional decisions and our actions. But it's our beliefs about our students that drive these decisions and actions. I've realized that awareness of my beliefs and intentionality in my actions are critical. Below are three areas of focus for holding and communicating high expectations for all students.

Area 1: Reflect on Your Expectations for Your Students

Think about each of your students. Could you divide them into categories, those you expect to be successful and those you expect to struggle?

What made you place students in each category? Was it their past performance? Was it their labels or language proficiency? Was it the neighborhoods from which they come?

Area 2: Reflect on Your Instructional Choices

Expectations are often communicated through differentiated treatment in the classroom. What kinds of tasks are you assigning to the students you listed in the two different categories? Do you give one group more choice in assignments? Do you ask questions or respond to answers differently? Do you give more or different types of feedback?

Area 3: Reflect on Your Interactions

Expectations may also be communicated through tone or affect. What kinds of interactions do you have with the students you listed in the two different categories? Do you get more easily frustrated with one group than the other? Are you less tolerant of off-task behavior with some students? Do you spend more time in conversation with some students? Do your actions suggest that you are more invested in some students?

These honest reflections are difficult, but understanding your beliefs and how those beliefs may influence your actions is a powerful path toward greater impact.

Notes and Works Cited

p. 55 Rosenthal, R., & Jacobson, L. (1968). Pygmalion in the classroom. *Urban Review, 3*(1), 16

p. 55 Rosenthal, R. (2003). *Pygmalion in the classroom : teacher expectation and pupils' intellectual development.* Crown House Publishing.

p. 57 Weinstein, R. S. (2002). *Reaching higher : the power of expectations in schooling.* Harvard University Press.

p. 60 Jackson, Y. (2011). *The pedagogy of confidence : inspiring high intellectual performance in urban schools.* Teachers College Press.

6

Lessons on Memorable Moments

Early on Monday morning, I sat down at my desk in the den to survey the notes and stories I collected over the weekend. The concepts of safe, seen, and stretched were evident in the stories shared by Lisa, Emilio, and Jay. The ways in which their memorable teachers connected with them and the ways in which those teachers expected more from them made a lasting impact on these former students. But something else in the data piqued my curiosity: many of the stories I had collected revolved around small, brief moments. The people I interviewed often described a teacher's specific words or actions. In the course of a semester or school year, these moments must have accounted for a tiny fraction of the time spent in a classroom, yet the memories of the moments persisted for decades.

I dug through my papers looking for one particular story. I pulled the page with Louise's story out of the pile on my desk and marveled at the specificity. Louise's recollection of Mr. Alexander's class was filled with small moments. "Mr. Alexander was my fifth grade teacher," Louise had shared. "He had an excitement for learning that was contagious and made every day in his class an adventure. With his tousled hair and tie flung over his shoulder (it was the '60s!) he knew how to create a memorable experience."

DOI: 10.4324/9781003122029-7

Louise recalled a disagreement about whether the girls or boys had first claim to the preferred kickball field at recess. "We did not get a lecture or reprimand for fussing. Instead, he taught us about our judicial system and then had us use that knowledge to conduct a trial to decide the issue. Even though this process took days, we enthusiastically researched and prepared our cases, called witnesses, and agreed to abide by the jury's decision."

Louise fondly remembered Mr. Alexander's passion for literature and the variety of classic stories, novels, and poetry he presented. "On overcast days, he would turn off the lights to set the mood for Edgar Allan Poe stories on the record player. We shivered as Fortunato was walled up in *The Cask of Amontillado* and when the murderer's guilty conscience heard the rhythmic thumping of his victim's heart in *The Tell-Tale Heart*." Louise remembered reading the poetry of Robert Frost and then listening to recordings of him reading his own works.

Louise recognized the vivid nature of her memories. "There are pictures of so many wonderful moments in Mr. Alexander's class imprinted in my mind, even all these years later. He taught us to think, to create, to listen, and to learn … And we loved him for it."

Memorable Moments

The detail in Louise's recollection spoke to the lasting nature of some moments. What made her memories of Mr. Alexander's class so enduring? Daniel Khaneman, a Nobel prize winner and researcher of behavioral economics, has long studied memory and experiences. According to Dr. Khaneman, our lives are just a string of moments, each lasting around three seconds. Therefore, we experience about 20,000 of these moments in a day. If we live to be 70, we will have experienced upwards of 500 million moments. What happens to all of them? Most of them simply disappear, with a few exceptions.

The moments that stick usually happen when we feel a sense of connection with others. Moments of unexpected joy or intimacy are often enduring. We also tend to remember the times when we felt engaged in purposeful action, when we were accomplishing something worthwhile. Conversely, moments of boredom or futility just fade away. And moments that are simply transactional don't stick.

Dr. Khaneman also suggests that, over the duration of an experience, we tend to remember the peak moments. Most of our time in a teacher's class may be forgettable, but we will remember that teacher as long as some moments are remarkable. To clarify, remarkable moments do not have to be dramatic or flashy, they just have to be meaningful. And as students, we create the meaning. In these instances of connection, inspiration, or immersion, we define ourselves. We come to see ourselves as members of a community, as learners and doers. We come to see ourselves as creators and makers. Maybe that is why we don't remember being taught, but we remember being transformed.

Suddenly, I heard my phone buzz from somewhere within the pile of papers. I had left a message for my colleague, Minka, a professor in the psychology department, asking if she had a few minutes for me. Her reply was short and sweet: "Always a minute for you. Come on over." I grabbed my list of questions and headed over to the north side of campus, just past the rose garden.

Memory and Identity

I found Minka in her office along with Jordan, a student assistant. I told them both about my project and shared a few of the stories. I explained the concepts of safe, seen, and stretched emerging from the data and asked the question I hoped Minka could answer. "With all of the moments that happen in a school day, in a school year, or even over the entirety of our schooling, why do we remember some of them so clearly?"

Minka (always one for challenging students) turned to Jordan. "What do you think?"

Jordan sat up in her chair. "I'm thinking about my former teachers. I would expect to remember the eccentric ones, but the ones I remember best were not particularly quirky. I'd have to say Mrs. Arbor was my favorite, and she was soft spoken and undramatic. It's like you said—I remember the way she made me feel. She made me feel important."

Jordan described her experience in Mrs. Arbor's classroom. "I am the youngest of four children. Growing up, my sister was a gifted pianist and both of my brothers excelled in sports. I was quiet and preferred reading to performing on a stage or field. At home, I always felt left out and left behind." Jordan described Mrs. Arbor's class as the one place she felt special. "Mrs. Arbor loved the same books I did, and we would sit and talk about the characters. She often recommended new titles she thought I would enjoy."

Then she recalled a specific incident. "On conference night, I sat between Mrs. Arbor and my parents, prepared for the usual explanation of test scores and grades. Instead, Mrs. Arbor pulled out a folder full of my written responses to the books I read. She told my parents that I was very insightful for my age. She pointed out my choice of words and phrases and complimented my ability to express my thoughts in writing. When the conference was over, I practically floated out of the room."

Jordan paused for a minute. "Now you have me wondering, too. I had so many good teachers. I went to so many conference nights with my parents. Why do I remember that moment more than others?"

Minka leaned toward Jordan and asked, "How old were you then?"

"I was in fifth grade. Probably ten."

Minka smiled. "What did that encounter tell you about who you were as a person?"

"I guess it reaffirmed that I was not an athlete or musician. I was a reader and writer. And for the first time, I felt like those skills were just as valuable."

"It was a moment that contributed to the formation of your identity," Minka said. "The time from age ten to twenty is ripe for memory encoding." Then she proceeded to explain something called the Reminiscence Bump to Jordan and me.

There is an abundance of evidence that people recall a disproportionate number of autobiographical memories from the time of early adolescence to early adulthood. Memory researcher David Rubin refers to this phenomenon as the Reminiscence Bump. According to Dr. Rubin, this period in our lives not only produces the greatest number of memories, but also the most vivid and most important. When older adults were asked to provide memories from any period in their lives, they showed a significant preference for events that happened from the ages of ten to twenty.

From a cognitive standpoint, early childhood is a time of rapid change. During periods of rapid change, many of the things we encounter are novel. Because of our increased effort to understand and make sense of our world, we may be less efficient at retrieving those memories. But the transition from childhood to adulthood is a time when rapid change is giving way to more stability. Increased stability makes cuing and retrieval easier. It seems the best situation for memory is a period where events are still novel but at a less rapid rate. Early adolescence typically offers a sprinkling of novelty rather than the deluge of early childhood, making it a time when we can better understand and organize the events of our lives in order to retrieve the memories of these events later.

Older adults who participated in memory studies also showed a greater preference for cultural and creative work to which they were exposed from early adolescence to early adulthood. This may be due to the fact that they were developing an understanding of these art forms during that stage of life. Memory researchers have found nostalgia proneness to be a significant predictor of preference for particular books, music, and movies. Given a choice, we tend to judge the creative work we consumed as teenagers to be the best. Additionally, the social and political events happening during this period of identity development have an impact on the way we view our world as adults. Our views and preferences often tie us to a generation or era.

With Minka's list of resources, readings, and recommendations in hand, I walked back across campus. In my head, I was making connections from the stories I had gathered to the memory research Minka shared. I thought about Louise's story, and the vivid memories of the creative works she encountered in Mr. Alexander's class. I recalled Jill's story and how discussions of world events in Mr. Christie's class shaped her views. I thought about the necessity of bringing creative works and current events into classrooms, and it occurred to me that art and issues aren't accompaniments to our students' learning—they are *essential* to their learning. These aren't nice additions to the curriculum, just pieces we pull in when we have time. Rather, creative works and current events are the elements from which students develop an understanding of themselves and their world.

Turning Points

On the way home, I remembered that Laura's Advanced Placement Literature students would be taking their exam tomorrow. Exam day (and the days leading up to it) are always stressful for her. I dialed her number and she picked up on the first ring. "Hey! How are you?"

"Other than being out of shape," I said, breathless from toting my books and notes across campus, "I'm fine. More importantly, how are you? How are you feeling?"

Laura talked about how proud she was of her students and how much they had grown as readers, as writers, as critical thinkers, as humans. "I hate how this one test is meant to assess months of learning, as if a single score could ever capture it." Laura listed some of the factors that could interfere in her students' performance: a romantic relationship ending, a grandparent dying, homelessness, illness, trauma, anxiety. "What breaks my heart most when they don't do well is their feeling they've disappointed me. I do my best to reduce the weight of it, but they know the stakes."

I listened and offered reassurance, as if words could alleviate the pressure. I shared a few of the stories I had gathered since we last spoke.

"Hearing the stories does help," she said. "The memories of your participants shine a light on what really matters long term. I needed that dose of inspiration. I'm sure other teachers could use it, too. Have you thought about publishing them? Maybe a blog?"

I promised to consider it and wished my friend an uneventful and successful testing day.

Back home, I settled into a chair in my dining room and looked at the stories spread across the table. I could see mounting evidence to support the importance of feeling safe, seen, and stretched in the classroom. But I was still trying to understand why some moments are particularly memorable. I reread a story at the top of the pile. It was a story told by an undergraduate student when I visited a colleague's class. Karen had invited me to talk to her group of music education majors about my project. Steven stayed behind after my presentation to tell me about his experience as a young child in school.

"I remember constantly getting into trouble in kindergarten for tapping on the table with my pencil," he began. "When my teacher took the pencil away, I just tapped with my fingers. My mom (tired of getting notes about it) tried to bribe me with a variety of treats. It was no use; I just couldn't help it."

Steven witnessed his teachers' increasing annoyance with his tapping as he progressed through school, resulting in a growing number of office referrals. "The assistant principal suggested tapping on my legs instead, but that wasn't satisfying without the sound."

He started second grade with a promise to his mom that he wouldn't get in trouble for tapping. "It was so difficult because I often started to tap my pencil without even realizing I was doing it."

A few weeks into second grade, Mrs. Merkle asked Steven to stay after school. "I was ready for the usual lecture, but instead, she asked me to take a walk. We walked to the middle school next to our elementary school. She led me into a big room with a piano and a variety of other instruments." It was her husband, Mr. Merkle's, room. Steven described the way Mr. Merkle held out two sticks and asked him to tap on his table. He smiled at Mrs. Merkle and taught Steven a few rhythms.

"The Merkles eventually convinced my mom to let me take drum lessons. I have been drumming ever since. It is the thing that makes me feel most alive," Steven said. "I will always be grateful to the Merkles for seeing a gift where others only saw an annoyance. I have shared my gift all over the country in a praise band. Now, I plan to share it with the students I will teach."

As I looked from Steven's story to the others in the pile, the pattern became clear. These were stories of change, stories of positive turning points in students' lives, and they had the same three movements: a prior state, a moment of transformation facilitated by a teacher's actions, and a subsequent new trajectory. Educational researcher Gad Yair studies turning points in the educational experiences of students. He describes these points as evidence of the capacity of teachers to make a real difference in students' lives. Out of all key educational experiences, students describe turning points as the most memorable. According to Dr. Yair, these moments are characterized by cognitive stimulation, emotional excitement, and self-discovery. The turning point stories in my data provided more evidence that students don't remember being taught; they remember being transformed. Turning points are powerful illustrations of the ways teachers shape students' lives.

The Birth of a Blog

I was pulled from my focus by the sudden, high-pitched barking of Winnie and Charlie. This type of barking could only mean one thing: Cailin was home. The dogs' excitement reached a fervor when both Cailin and Jake walked in the door. I couldn't blame the dogs. Cailin is like sunshine; she changes the energy of a room. Her boyfriend, Jake, is much the same. Together, they are double sunshine, twice the joy and twice the light.

Cailin and Jake both attended the University of South Florida, an institution with over 50,000 students and a campus full of activity, night and day. About twice a month they made the 40-minute drive to the tranquility of Lakeland. They greeted the pups and walked over to examine the papers strewn across the table. As they read a few of the stories, I shared Laura's idea about a blog.

Jake was a marketing major, and he was all in for building a website, but there was one problem: my project didn't yet have a name. I had no idea how to come up with a name for a blog, so Jake began asking a series of questions. "What do teachers use to change students' lives? What tools did your teachers use with you?"

I thought about it. "Chalk … lots of chalk. And chances … lots of chances."

"I love that! Chalk and Chances. It's simple, yet memorable."

Before I knew it, the Chalk and Chances website was born.

Cailin, who had been giving input on colors and design, finally called for a break in the action. "I'm starving. Can we hit Fresco's for dinner?"

It was the least I could do for my uncompensated marketing and design team. Once seated at our favorite outdoor table, I asked for their advice again. "I need to collect more stories. There are still so many gaps, so much I don't yet understand about teacher impact. I've collected stories around Lakeland, but I'd like to visit a place with a different vibe, maybe a younger crowd."

Jake turned to Cailin. "The Bull Market. Don't you think your mom should do the Bull Market?"

Cailin practically bounced out of her chair. "Yes—that would be so fun! Mom, you should do it!" I wasn't so sure, but Jake took out his laptop and pulled up pictures of the weekly market in the field by the university's student center. And before I knew it, I was registered for my next adventure in data collection. Luckily, I had a few weeks to prepare.

Applying Lessons on Memorable Moments

The stories students tell about events in the past are reconstructions. They filter these memories through the experiences and understanding gained since the memorable event. Therefore, some memories grow stronger and more meaningful over time. Often, these memories contain personal messages that become guideposts and continue to influence students throughout their lives. As teachers, we can't force memorable moments to happen, but we can create the conditions under which they are most likely to occur.

Area 1: Create Shared Experiences

Memorable experiences are most often shared experiences. Consider how you can integrate the content you teach into a shared experience. How can your students work together through a purposeful struggle, like a problem or puzzle to solve? How can you provide ways for students to find meaning in the content together, perhaps through cooperative projects?

Area 2: Explore Students' Identities

Students create their own personal narratives to explain events in their lives, how those events are connected, and why they happened. How can you give students space to create and share personal experiences? Young people are always seeking clues about their identities. How can you help them understand their identities and affirm their value in the classroom community?

Area 3: Creating Conditions for Transformation

Transformations (or turning points) are most likely to occur if students can release past failures or stigmas. How can you communicate the possibility of a fresh start to a student who has struggled? Turning points and transformation are also more likely when students sense enthusiasm and commitment in their teachers. How can you convey a sense of enthusiasm and commitment about helping your students reach their potential?

Notes and Works Cited

p. 64   Khaneman, D. & Riis, J. (2005). Living and thinking about it: Two perspectives on life. *The Science of Well-Being*, 285–304. Oxford University Press.

p. 67   Rubin, D. C., & Berntsen, D. (2012). *Understanding autobiographical memory : Theories and approaches*. Cambridge University Press.

p. 68   Yair Gad. (2009). Cinderellas and ugly ducklings: Positive turning points in students' educational careers—exploratory evidence and a future agenda. *British Educational Research Journal, 35*(3), 351–370.

7

Lessons on Community

I'm ashamed to admit that two weeks had passed since my data collection day at the farmers' market, and I still had Jack's tent in the back of my car. I was feeling especially guilty because Jack is the best neighbor and citizen I know. He is active in our college alumni group, President of Rotary, and involved in more charitable organizations than I could count. If service or good works are happening in Lakeland, Jack is surely present. When I pulled into his driveway, he came right out to help me. "How did it go?"

"The weather was perfect," I answered. "Dozens of people stopped to talk about their teachers. The willingness to share such personal memories still surprises me."

"Well, you are pretty intimidating and unapproachable," Jack laughed. "What are you finding out?"

I shared a few of the stories and explained the concepts of safe, seen, and stretched.

"You know, that doesn't just apply to teachers. All kinds of leaders, even parents, could learn from those models."

I agreed with Jack and told him I believed the project was helping me become a better parent, colleague, and friend.

"Do you ever give presentations about your project? I'm asking because we're always looking for speakers for our Rotary meetings. We support our local schools, and I think your topic would interest the members."

DOI: 10.4324/9781003122029-8

Although the thought of talking in front of business people made me nervous, I agreed. I had been wondering how non-educators would receive the project. Besides, I owed Jack for a two-week tent rental.

Classroom Communities

I left Jack's house and headed straight to Edge Hall to teach a graduate class. As students were coming in, I told them about my opportunity to speak to the Rotary Club.

"I would be petrified," Cammie responded, unpacking her backpack. "I can talk in front of kids all day, but talking in front of grown-ups is completely different." The other students agreed. As a former principal and now professor, I was used to talking to educators. These were my people; we spoke the same language. Business people seemed intimidating. I understood my students' fear.

I couldn't have planned a better segue into the content of that class session. Talking about the Rotary Club led right into our focus for the evening: building a sense of community in our schools. I started by asking my students to recall a time when they felt part of a community in school. Kristen spoke up first.

"Mrs. Thomas was my fourth grade teacher. She created such a caring culture in our classroom. She named it Thomasville, and we all became official citizens."

Kristen described the way Mrs. Thomas distributed weekly paychecks for completing tasks and doing jobs. "We paid rent and paid fines when we violated the rules. At the end of each month, we could use our paychecks to purchase tickets for special activities, like movies or art projects."

Being a citizen of Thomasville, Kristen explained, taught her the importance of accountability and collective responsibility. "I learned that there are consequences for my actions, both positive and negative. I learned that, in a community, we take care of those in need. When one of our classmates was out for weeks with a broken leg, Mrs. Thomas announced that we could each contribute a small amount so he could attend the movie—and everybody did."

The graduate students and I all marveled at the ingenuity of Mrs. Thomas. We admired the way she taught life lessons without lecturing, and the way she built a community. I then introduced the class to the partnership between educational researcher Jerome Freiberg and psychologist Carl Rogers. The two had observed many classrooms where students seemed more like tourists than citizens, simply passing through without involvement, commitment, or belonging. Together, they sought to train teachers in strategies for creating classroom communities where cooperation, participation, and support are the cornerstones. These two researchers viewed the ideal classroom as neither fully student-centered nor teacher-centered, but rather person-centered. Dr. Freiberg and Dr. Rogers believed that students developed self-discipline cooperatively with their teachers and peers. They advocated for students contributing to their classrooms and schools in meaningful ways, rather than just passively moving through school.

Building a classroom community starts with an agreement acknowledged by all members of the community (including the teacher) specifying rules based on mutual needs. Along with that commitment is a focus on caring, signified by recognizing and responding to others' needs. Displays of student work and celebrations of students' milestones create a family atmosphere. Cooperation is an ongoing characteristic of a classroom community. Working cooperatively creates a sense of knowing each other that leads to trusting each other. And working cooperatively also ensures the division of tasks and shared responsibilities. The totality of these efforts is a classroom where students feel a sense of ownership and a sense of belonging.

Classroom communities embody the concepts of safe, seen, and stretched. Being supported by both the teacher and peers creates a safe space for acknowledging a need, seeking help, and taking a risk. Being accepted as a member of the community without having to hide, adjust, or fit into a box provides a sense of being safe and known. Being entrusted with responsibilities for daily classroom operations builds a sense of competence and confidence. Teachers who intentionally create the conditions in which students feel safe, seen, and stretched build a culture of community and have a powerful impact on students' academic, social, and emotional growth.

In-groups and Out-groups

As I carried my books back to my office after class, my phone buzzed with a text message: *Did you eat? If not, meet me at Buck Stop.* Skipping lunch was catching up with me, signified by my grumbling stomach. The smoke from the Buck Stop grill drew me to the middle of campus where Brian had already ordered a hamburger for himself and a grilled chicken sandwich for me. We grabbed one of the tables under the big oak tree. "I finally took the tent back to Jack," I confessed as I unwrapped my sandwich.

"Thanks for returning it." Brian peeled the pickles off his burger. "How's Jack doing?"

"Jack's great. He asked me to speak to his Rotary Club, but I'm a little anxious about talking to business people."

Brian finished his bite of burger. "You do realize you're married to a professor in the School of Business, right? And you have many friends who are business professors. So, what's up with that?"

"I just don't think they'll get it. They're all about making a profit, taking big risks, and beating the competition. I don't think they'll care about how teachers make a difference in students' lives."

"Okay, is this true about the people you know?" he challenged. "Is this true about Jack? Or, is this just a stereotype about business people in general? Aren't you the one who gets upset when people promulgate negative stereotypes about teachers?"

Brian wasn't wrong. I get worked up when I hear teachers described as lazy, resistant to accountability, or unwilling to change. The people who describe teachers this way usually tell a different story about their own teachers or their children's teachers, but they're quick to criticize teachers in general.

PDK International (a professional organization for educators) conducts an annual poll to assess the public's attitude toward schools. In a recent poll, 70% of parents gave their child's school an A or B grade, while just 19% of respondents gave top grades to schools in general. Teachers and schools continue to suffer from a deficit in public perception from outsiders.

Psychologist Patricia Linville has spent decades studying how we make appraisals of people from in-groups and out-groups. In-group members share a common characteristic, such as ethnicity or occupation. We tend to perceive members of our in-group as unique and complex individuals, perhaps because we have a larger collection of interactions with people from our own group. On the other hand, we tend to have fewer interactions with those outside our group. Therefore, our impressions of out-group members may be heavily influenced by stereotypes, seeing all members as having the same behaviors, attitudes, and values. This may partially explain the negative narratives about teachers from those outside the profession.

Professor and author Steven Jones suggests that the story of failing public schools has long circulated among legislators, business groups, media personalities, and citizens in general. The central figures in this story, the teachers, are blamed for this failure. Dr. Jones suggests that the people (education outsiders) telling the story include enough facts (reliable or not) to make it seem true. The worst part of this story is the way it resonates emotionally, drawing a sense of betrayal and resentment toward teachers. How could they care so little about the well-being of children? Sometimes the story of failing schools is told openly, but often it is hidden behind reform efforts. The narrative suggests educators need outsiders to fix the broken system.

As a member of the education in-group, I know educators are doing the best they can with limited resources and increasing responsibilities. Perhaps my opportunity to talk with members of the education out-group could change the story. Maybe I could help them understand the real challenges teachers are facing. Could delivering my message to business leaders and community groups alter the narrative? Even better, could I convince them to advocate for policies that help rather than harm teachers? I became determined to try.

I finished my sandwich deep in thought and looked over at Brian. "You make a good argument."

He smiled. "Say it."

"You have a point."

Brian leaned in. "You're so close."

"Okay. You're right."

He jumped up and raised his fists in victory, and continued to celebrate as he cleared off our table.

Community Partnerships

On the day of the Rotary event, I was prepared but still apprehensive. My presentation had been scrubbed of educational jargon and had been designed with education outsiders in mind. My memories of my favorite teacher, Mrs. Russell, would be the opener. I would then ask the Rotarians to remember their favorite teachers and how those teachers made an impact on their lives. I would also ask them to advocate for policies and legislation based on their best teachers, not on some generalized story about teachers. A few deep breaths in the parking lot calmed my nerves before I headed into the meeting.

After Jack introduced me, the whole presentation felt like a blur. Grateful for the enthusiastic response, I stayed behind for almost an hour to shake hands, answer questions, and most importantly, to receive the Rotarians' stories about their teachers. Many admitted they hadn't thought about their teachers in years. The last one in line was Jackson, a local business owner who felt compelled to tell me about his middle school teacher, Mr. Ernest.

"I grew up in a neighborhood without many fathers," Jackson confessed. "Some of them were in jail, some were dead, and some were just gone, like mine. It's hard for a boy to grow up without a man at home, but my mother and grandmother did the best they could."

Jackson told me that Mr. Ernest, his computer teacher, worried about the boys in the neighborhood and decided to start a club for eighth graders to help them prepare for high school and beyond. The group was named The Young Men of Distinction. "In our meetings, he taught us how to shake hands, how to look people in the eye when speaking, and how to politely correct someone who mispronounced our names. That was real important to Mr. Ernest, that we were proud of our names." Jackson described the way Mr. Ernest invited community leaders in to talk. They listened to the boys, too, and it made Jackson feel important.

"One day, Mr. Ernest got a store downtown to donate a bunch of ties," Jackson explained. "He taught us how to tie a perfect knot. When we could demonstrate it to him on our own, we got to pick out a tie to keep. Mr. Ernest laid a foundation for my success. He helped me understand that wherever I go, I must represent my family, my school, and myself well. I'm trying to teach those lessons to my own son now. And just last week, I taught him how to make a perfect tie knot."

Jackson ended my time at the Rotary meeting on a high note, and with something important to consider about teacher impact. Just as teachers can't bear the sole blame for failures, they also can't be solely responsible for success. Mr. Ernest lived the proverb, *It takes a village to raise a child*. He understood the importance of community partnerships. Educational researcher Anthony Bryk has provided a myriad of evidence supporting the benefits of community engagement in schools. According to Dr. Bryk, strong school–community partnerships can provide support and resources beyond what is typically available in schools. The relationships among teachers, students, parents, and community members influence whether students attend school regularly and whether they willingly engage in challenging academic tasks. Relationships between teachers and the community also impact the ability of teachers to access and use external resources and support. In other words, significant school improvement is unlikely without a high degree of relational trust.

When teachers, administrators, and other school personnel are intentional about the frequency and quality of their interactions with community members, they create the knowing that leads to trusting. And trust is strengthened when partnerships are mutually beneficial—when needs are satisfied for both sides. Frequent reciprocal communication and an inviting school culture are necessary for engaging community partners. With an agreement on placing the needs of students first, mutual dependency, and high expectations for all, schools and communities working together can create better outcomes for students.

Inclusive Communities

News travels fast in Lakeland, and I soon found myself making the rounds as a speaker at community group events. I had to admit I was enjoying the opportunity to talk to a broader audience about the ways teachers impact lives, and these opportunities always yielded more stories, more data for analysis. With enthusiasm (and honestly, still a bit of nerves), I headed to speak to a local church group. They were a welcoming crowd and made connections between teaching and their own dedication to serving others. Many of the church members shared stories after my talk. One of the church members, Amy, told me about Mrs. Deen, the third grade teacher who taught her about compassion and grace.

"When I was in third grade, a new student joined our class," Amy began. "Our teacher, Mrs. Deen, prepared us for Aaron's arrival. She explained that he had something called Down syndrome, a condition that happened before he was born. She told us that Aaron's speech may be hard to understand and that he may at times become frustrated or forget the rules while he adjusts to being in our classroom."

Amy admitted that, at first, all of the kids were very curious about Aaron, especially when he acted impulsively. Mrs. Deen taught them to talk to Aaron softly and calmly when he did something wrong. She told them to remind him of the rules and show him the right way to do things. "Over time, Aaron got better at following the rules, and we got better at understanding what he was trying to say."

Amy described the way Mrs. Deen assigned students to help Aaron during different times of the day. Amy helped him during reading. They practiced flash cards and she helped him pick books from the library shelf. He liked Amy reading to him, but he didn't like writing. "Holding the pencil was hard for Aaron, and sometimes, he would push the pencil and papers off his desk. Just like Mrs. Deen instructed, I would softly tell Aaron that we could take a break if he picked his things up," Amy explained.

Occasionally, she admitted, a student from another class would ask what was wrong with Aaron. "Mrs. Deen always responded, 'Nothing is wrong with him. His brain just works a little differently than yours does.'" Amy and her classmates learned to say the same thing to other kids. They became very protective of Aaron.

Amy smiled. "I know Aaron learned so much from being in our class. By the end of the year, he was speaking more clearly, reading better, and making friends. And we grew more confident from sharing the responsibility for helping him. Even the toughest kids learned to be kinder because of Aaron."

Amy revealed that she is now a pediatric nurse. When parents receive a difficult diagnosis, she assures them that their child isn't broken or damaged but that their child's brain or body just works differently. Amy hugged me goodbye and then turned back to add, "A child with a brain or a body that works differently can bring blessings and lessons for everyone in the community."

Amy's story spoke to the importance of inclusive communities. The way a teacher treats a child with challenges in the classroom has an impact on all of the learners in that classroom. Treating a student with respect and compassion while gently holding the student accountable builds trust, not just with that student but with all students. Seeing a struggling student treated with respect provides a feeling of safety, a reassurance that perfection is not a necessary requirement for belonging. Recognizing the strengths in all students, especially those with different abilities, communicates the innate value of all members of the community.

Sue Briggs, an expert on exceptional needs, describes inclusion as a means for making the school more responsive to the diverse needs of all learners. A school that is good for students with exceptional needs tends to be good for everyone. Successful inclusion requires teachers to consider ways to make activities more accessible, to promote social interaction, and to help students become more independent. All students have aspirations, and school can be a bridge to reaching those goals and dreams.

Teachers may experience initial fears or feelings of inadequacy when preparing for a student with significant needs. They may worry about maintaining discipline, communicating with the student, or attending to the student's medical needs. Strong and supportive partnerships with parents, service providers, and colleagues can alleviate teachers' fears and ensure success. Multi-disciplinary teams are vital to successful inclusion. When each member brings skills, knowledge, a willingness to collaborate, and the determination to solve problems, the student wins. In an inclusive classroom, everyone wins. The included student becomes more proficient socially and academically. The teacher has an opportunity to be more creative and innovative. And peers have the opportunity to develop appreciation for diversity and a sense of collective responsibility.

An Unexpected Opportunity

I had just gotten back in the house when the phone rang. It was a number and a voice I didn't recognize. "This is Tim Totten, organizer of TEDx Eustis. We've read about your research on memorable teachers, and we've chosen you to be a speaker at our next event."

I uttered some jumbled words of appreciation and asked for more information.

"The event will be held at the Old Bay State Theatre. You'll need to prepare a 15- to 18-minute talk. No note cards and, preferably, no slides."

I felt a wave of nausea begin and walked into the den to sit down. Being on a stage with no notes and no slides was way outside my comfort zone. But then my eyes went to the glass apple on my desk. I didn't even need to call my mom to know what she would tell me to do. My mom believed a person could learn to do almost anything with a bit of research and effort. Before the internet, she would be at the library, checking out books on faux paint finishes or sewing machine repair. Surely there was a club or a coach or someone who could help me speak on a stage without blanking out, or worse, passing out.

Then I heard Tim say something reassuring, "Remember, TEDx is about an idea worth spreading. You'll be sharing an idea, not putting on a show." The remarkable ways teachers make an impact on students' lives was definitely an idea worth spreading. So, I said yes to Tim. I would figure out how to deliver that idea later—there was no time to fret about it that evening as tomorrow was my day at the Bull Market, and I needed to prepare.

Applying Lessons on Community

As I visit schools, I'm struck by the differences in the climates and cultures of classrooms. A room full of disengaged, indifferent students may be quiet and under control, but it is far from joyful. Contrast that with a classroom community built on trust and cooperation. There is an energy in that room, a happy hum. I could stay there all day, and I'm certain students feel the same. Below are three areas of focus for creating a classroom community.

Area 1: Create a Classroom of Citizens

Cooperation, participation, and shared responsibility are the cornerstones of a classroom community. These are the keys to turning students from tourists to citizens, along with the following reflective questions.

Where are additional opportunities to involve students in the creation of norms and expectations in your classroom?

Where are additional opportunities for involving students in daily classroom operations?

How could you encourage students to recognize and respond to the needs of others with care and support?

Area 2: Developing Community Partnerships

Business and community members can provide additional resources, enrichment opportunities, and role models for students. An inviting school culture as well as the ability to communicate and collaborate are essential to successful community partnerships.

How can you keep the community informed about the happenings in your classroom or school?

Could you use newsletters or social media more effectively to inform and engage community members?

How can you elicit and use feedback from community members for continuous improvement?

Area 3: Creating an Inclusive Classroom

All children need acceptance, belonging, and a sense of community, regardless of their abilities, needs, or backgrounds. Inclusion is about being responsive to those different needs and providing appropriate support.

How can you help your students understand and value diversity?

How can you facilitate a culture of collective responsibility in which students help and support each other?

How can you work more collaboratively with colleagues and parents to better serve all students?

Notes and Works Cited

p. 76   Rogers, C. R., & Freiberg, H. J. (1994). *Freedom to learn, 3rd ed.* Merrill/Macmillan College Publishing Co.

p. 78   The 50th Annual PDK Poll of the Public's Attitudes toward the Public Schools. Teaching: Great respect, dwindling appeal. (2018). *Phi Delta Kappan, 100*(1).

p. 78   Linville, P. W., & Jones, E. E. (1980). Polarized appraisals of out-group members. *Journal of Personality and Social Psychology, 38*(5), 689–703.

p. 78   Jones, S. P. (2015). *Blame teachers: The emotional reasons for educational reform*. Information Age Publishing.

p. 80   Bryk, A., & Schneider, B. (2002). *Trust in schools : A core resource for improvement*. Russell Sage Foundation.

p. 82   Briggs, S. (2016). *Meeting special educational needs in primary classrooms: Inclusion and how to do it. 2nd Edition*. David Fulton Publishers.

8

Lessons on Identity

Brian was teaching the morning of the Bull Market, so I headed for the University of South Florida on my own. The market would be set up with tents and tables for the vendors, which meant I could travel light. During the drive, I wondered how this event would compare with my day at the Lakeland Downtown Farmers' Market. The older crowd enjoyed reminiscing about their school experiences. Would this younger crowd take the time to stop and share a story? Concerned that university students may not be eager to talk about their teachers, I did make a stop for mini candy bars on the way. Perhaps a big bowl of chocolate would bring the youth to my booth.

It was still early in the morning when I pulled into the parking lot, but I could already hear the hip hop music coming from the speakers over the hill. By the time I reached the field in front of the student center, the market was buzzing. A student volunteer helped me find my booth, located between a gourmet popsicle vendor and guide dog puppies in training. It was a perfect spot, and I decided I might not need the chocolate after all.

A Sense of Worth

As I finished setting up, a young man asked if he could set his coffee on my table while he played with the puppies next door. When he returned, he paused to read my sign. "I'm Drew,"

DOI: 10.4324/9781003122029-9

he said. "I can tell you about one of my teachers." I gratefully listened to the first story of the day as Drew told me about Mrs. Perkins, the high school teacher with high expectations.

"Mrs. Perkins was my Advanced Placement Literature teacher during my senior year in high school," he began. "It was a challenging class, but she found creative ways to encourage her students. She had a box of pencils with a personalized message printed on each: 'Mrs. Perkins is proud of me.' When a student accomplished something impressive, Mrs. Perkins would bestow a pencil."

Drew admitted seniors are too cool for most classroom celebrations, but they all coveted the *Perkins Pencil*. "Mrs. Perkins was undeniably kind, but she was not easily impressed. It was a real honor to receive a pencil. I remember receiving mine when I achieved a high score on a practice test. I used it sparingly so that I wouldn't sharpen it past the words printed on its side."

Drew remembered feeling mixed emotions on the last day of class. He was ready to leave high school but felt anxious about starting the next chapter. "I was going to a college far from home, and I wasn't sure that I was ready for college-level work. Mrs. Perkins, as usual, knew what her students needed to hear. She reminded us that we had worked hard and learned much. She assured us that we were well-prepared."

Drew described organizing his bedroom and packing for college over the summer. While cleaning out his backpack, he found a pencil in one of the pockets. He picked it up and read the words, "Mrs. Perkins is proud of me." The pencil now has a special place in Drew's dorm room. "It helps me feel more confident, and it's the perfect pencil for all of the tests to come."

As Drew headed off to class, I considered the significance of the *Perkins Pencil*. It wasn't the pencil itself that the students coveted; it was what the pencil represented. Psychologist Martin Covington is known for his research on student motivation and achievement. He suggests that a student's self-worth is related to perceptions of academic ability. Therefore, all students are driven to protect their sense of competence. According to Dr. Covington, there is a fundamental conflict underlying the need for achievement. The conflict arises when a student's desire for success clashes with the desire to avoid failure.

The way students resolve this conflict depends upon their achievement orientations. Success-oriented individuals tend to select tasks for which the probability of success and the likelihood of failure are about equal. This provides them with enough successes to stay motivated without cheapening the accomplishment with an easy victory. Success-oriented students develop helpful strategies they can bring from one challenge to the next. Failure-avoiding individuals, on the other hand, tend to select tasks that are too easy or far too difficult, reinforcing the feelings of failure they were trying to avoid. They also employ self-defeating strategies, such as procrastinating or making excuses. Their failure, then, can be blamed on lack of effort rather than ability.

How can teachers help students resolve this conflict between the desire to succeed and the desire to avoid failure? How can teachers help students employ success-oriented strategies rather than failure-avoidant strategies? It starts with creating a non-competitive environment and a focus on effort and growth. Acknowledging only the highest score or best performance can leave many students feeling defeated. Not everyone can be the best, but everyone can improve and grow. There is a sweet spot between recognizing only the top scorers and giving out participation trophies. Teachers can facilitate students' feelings of competence and worth by recognizing successes achieved through effort and persistence, rather than rewarding easily achievable success.

The *Perkins Pencil* was a symbol of hard-earned achievement. By recognizing her students' success in difficult tasks, Mrs. Perkins reinforced their sense of competence and worth. She helped form their identities as learners. She helped them see themselves as scholars who could succeed in a demanding academic environment. By providing challenging content and tasks, Mrs. Perkins stretched her students. Teaching them strategies for tackling those tasks and providing support created a sense of safety. Recognizing their achievements helped them feel seen. By creating a classroom culture where they felt safe, seen, and stretched, Mrs. Perkins set her students up for future success.

A Sense of Belonging

By noon, the popsicle vendor started selling, and I had collected twelve more stories. I was gaining a better understanding of the university students' perspectives on their k-12 teachers. Just as I was contemplating the purchase of a strawberry popsicle, a group of young women approached. They were all wearing Greek letters identifying their sorority. Allie was the first one to volunteer a story. She shared fond memories of her high school astronomy teacher, Mr. McVie.

"I was not really interested in astronomy," she said. "I needed a science credit, and Mr. McVie's class fit into my schedule. Within the first two minutes of class, it was clear that he had two passions: astronomy and classic rock. Mr. McVie combined these two passions in a way that made all of us fall in love with comets and Led Zeppelin. He would often invite us to meet in the field behind the school late at night where he would assemble his telescope collection. Of course, he would also bring his portable speakers. I think everyone should experience a meteor shower accompanied by the Rolling Stones' greatest hits at least once." Allie recalled being out in the field, seeing planets and constellations she never knew existed.

She confessed that the stars help her feel less lonely in her new university home. "Now that I'm in college and my high school friends are far away, I love to go outside and look up at the night sky. It makes me feel like we're all still connected. It also reminds me of how big the universe is and how small my problems really are. Sometimes as I look at the stars, I even play some Rolling Stones in honor of Mr. McVie."

Allie's story reminded me of a study conducted by Laura Pittman and Adeya Richmond. These researchers examined the impact of high school belonging on students' college adjustment. Students' reports of belonging during their time in high school were significant predictors of academic performance and psychological wellness in their early college years. This was persistent even after controlling for other demographic and relationship factors. A sense of belonging was also a protective factor for students who enter college with a higher risk of dropping out, such as first-generation college students. Attending college requires students to make multiple, simultaneous adjustments, including changes in living arrangements, academic expectations, friendship networks, and levels of independence. Bringing a sense of belonging from their high school experience can create a feeling of stability for students, as well as a pathway for developing a sense of belonging in the college community.

Past feelings of connectedness with a school community are likely to lead to a greater sense of belonging in future school communities. The sense of belonging we cultivate in k-12 settings will serve our students well beyond high school. School connection encompasses the student's perceptions of fitting in, as well as commitment to the school community, commitment to making an effort in the community, and a sense of one's effort and abilities being recognized and appreciated by others. In other words, a sense of belonging motivates students to fully engage. A connection has been found between school belonging and better academic performance, better social-emotional functioning, and lower levels of depression. Cultivating this connectedness serves our students well both now and in the future.

Mr. McVie used his passion for rockets and rock music to engage his students in the content, and he created memorable experiences for the classroom community related to the content. The result for students was a collective sense of identity as members of a learning community. Allie tapped into these memories as a way to feel grounded during a time of great transition. She also used the memories of Mr. McVie's class as a model for engaging in her new home. In this way, Allie's high school experiences helped her hang on to a sense of feeling safe and seen while she continued to stretch.

Future Teachers

By the time I finished with Allie and her sorority sisters, Cailin's classes had ended for the day. Visiting with her was a welcome break, and I loved meeting her friends, who were also education majors. I asked them about why they chose to become teachers.

Almost all of them credited a teacher who made a difference in their lives, and they talked about their desires to make an impact on the lives of their future students. I also asked them how others react to their choice of major. Their answers were discouraging but not surprising.

The concern their families expressed is consistent with national trends. In the 50th Annual PDK International poll to assess the public's attitude toward schools, 54% of parents across the United States said they would not want their child to become a teacher. They cited inadequate pay, lack of respect, and dangerous working conditions as reasons for discouraging their child from pursuing a career in teaching. As parents, we don't want our children to suffer. As educators, it's disheartening to think that teaching has come to be associated with such suffering and unfavorable working conditions.

I was curious about how other college students reacted to the choice of education as a major. Emily spoke up first. "They think it's an easy major. They think we just color and cut things out," she said. "What they don't realize is the amount of time we spend in classrooms. We do field experiences throughout our courses, and we might be the only major that requires a full-time, unpaid internship."

Emily described the challenge of applying the concepts from her classes in a real classroom. "Last year, I was in a third grade classroom every Wednesday. This one student, Zander, challenged me all day. He refused to work and would do the opposite of everything I said. I worked with my professors and my cooperating teacher to come up with some strategies. They all told me to be patient and consistent. By the end of the year, he was a different kid. He even wrote me a note to thank me for teaching him."

I recognized the look in Emily's eyes. She was hooked. I knew she would spend the rest of her teaching career chasing those breakthrough moments. All of the frustration and exhaustion fade away the moment a student finally gets the concept or changes an unhelpful habit. That feeling is intensified when students recognize a teacher's role in their success with genuine expressions of gratitude. I'm not saying those moments negate the need for a livable wage or safer facilities, but they do keep teachers going.

Beyond Academic Content

Jake caught up with Cailin at my booth after he finished his duties as a marketing intern. True to his nature, he was soon sending a steady stream of friends my way. Just before the market closed, he sent Kevin to tell me about Mr. Cribbs, the fourth grade teacher who taught him the value of collaboration.

"I was a kid who loved any game that involved a ball, so I lived for recess," Kevin told me. "The best thing about fourth grade was going to go to the upper grades' playground, the one with the volleyball net. Every day after lunch, we would organize a volleyball game. Some of us would dominate every game. We spiked the ball as hard as we could or tried to hit it so the other side couldn't hit it back. Most of the girls would quit early, and some of the boys would get hurt."

Then Kevin acknowledged the genius of his teacher. "One day, Mr. Cribbs bet us 15 extra minutes of recess that we couldn't keep the ball going back and forth over the net 50 times. Then he added one stipulation: everyone had to touch the ball at least once." Kevin explained how they started to hit the ball so that other kids could hit it back. They even started to teach the other kids how to hit it up high with their fingertips. All of his classmates would count loudly together every time the ball went over the net.

"We got the ball across the net 62 consecutive times once. We named it The Infinite Game because we tried to keep it going as long as we could. It became our favorite thing to do at recess, and the whole class played." Kevin admitted that working together was way more fun than dominating the game, a lesson that would continue to stick with him.

"Now I'm an engineering student. It's a tough major, and many students drop out. Early in my first class, I organized a study group. We help each other; we make sure everyone succeeds. I could have focused on making the highest grade, but

I decided to play The Infinite Game. I'll be a better engineer for it. I thank Mr. Cribbs for teaching me the value of collaborating."

Kevin's story illustrates the importance of developing skills that are necessary for success in the workplace—skills like the ability to work with a team. The Association of American Colleges and Universities sponsored a survey of over 300 employers to identify their hiring priorities. Nearly all of the respondents agreed that the ability to think critically, communicate clearly, and solve complex problems is more important than a candidate's undergraduate major. Employers also identified a focus on innovation as critical to their success, indicating that the challenges their employees face today are more complex and require a broader skill set than ever before. The survey revealed that more than 80% of employers look for collaboration skills in new hires, but only 40% view new graduates as prepared to work collaboratively in teams.

How can teachers ensure that students are prepared for the demands of today's work environments? Just putting students in groups with a task is not enough. Intentionally teaching the foundations of collaboration (communicating with others, resolving conflicts, and managing tasks) is a good place to start. A focus on collaboration has many benefits for students in addition to preparation for employment. Educational researcher Joshua Adams found the more students of different abilities worked in collaborative groups, the more subject knowledge increased for all students. Leadership skills also grew in all students, regardless of social status. And, since reasoning skills are forged in language, conceptual relationships are deepened through group discussions.

This period of late adolescence and early adulthood is a prime time for identity development, when students discover who they are socially, ideologically, and vocationally. A personal identity provides a cohesive sense of self, from which students can make better decisions. A sense of worthiness, a sense of belonging, and a set of skills necessary for succeeding in their work can help students see themselves as competent and prepared. Young adults who have committed to some aspects of identity also experience greater life satisfaction and less anxiety. By providing a safe place for them to explore aspects of their identity and by communicating acceptance through this process, teachers shape their students' lives for good.

Now and Later

I finally indulged in a strawberry popsicle and some puppy-cuddling just before the market closed. It was a productive day of story collecting, leaving me with much to ponder on the drive home. I thought about the way teaching is both grounded in the present moment and focused on the future. As teachers, we create spaces where our students feel safe, seen, and stretched. We accept and appreciate them just as they are, but we also prepare them for what is coming. Whether that future is in higher education or a vocation, a sense of worth and belonging will help them navigate the transition. The identity we help them form as learners today will propel them through challenges tomorrow.

I thought about my own efforts to stay mindful of the present moment while preparing for the future. I didn't want to leave Cailin and Jake behind, but I had some serious preparation to do. The TEDx event was quickly approaching, and I was not yet ready. Lucky for me I'd found Coach Jen, and she was working to shape my identity as a speaker. I needed to see it in my mind before I could be it on the stage. Just as it was for the students I'd met at the Bull Market, this identity development work was not easy. But I had a feeling it would be worth it.

Applying Lessons on Identity

Adolescents and young adults are wrestling with the question, *Who am I?* Their answers to that question are heavily influenced by their school experiences. Identity is related to one's sense of worthiness, competence, and belonging. As teachers, we can shape the way students see themselves now and into the future. Below are three areas of focus related to identity development.

Within each area are practices and questions for reflection to help you positively shape your students' lives.

Area 1: A Sense of Worth

For many students, a sense of worth in school is tied to academic performance. Think about the way your students view themselves as learners. Are they focused on their rank among their peers or on their own growth?

How can you recognize their effort and perseverance?

Students who seek to avoid failure often employ unhelpful strategies, such as procrastination, lack of effort, or excuses. How can you help them overcome that fear and replace unhelpful habits with strategies for success?

Area 2: A Sense of Belonging

A sense of belonging in school is associated with better academic, social, and emotional outcomes for students. This connectedness within a school community also helps students transition into future school settings. High school students who experienced this feeling of belonging in high school transitioned more easily into college life. How can you facilitate a feeling of belonging and commitment to the school community for your students? How can you inspire your students' willingness to invest in the school community? How can you help all students feel safe and seen within the school community?

Area 3: A Sense of Competence and Preparedness

Succeeding in school and in life requires a set of skills beyond rote learning and memorization. Students who can collaboratively solve problems and innovate have a clear advantage. How can you intentionally teach students to communicate, collaborate, and solve problems? What experiences can you provide to help them practice these skills? How can you provide feedback and support as students develop these skills? How can you help students hold a vision of themselves as successful in the vocations to which they aspire?

Notes and Works Cited

p. 88   Covington, M. V., von Hoene, L. M., & Voge, D. J. (2017). *Life beyond grades: Designing college courses to promote intrinsic motivation.* Cambridge University Press.

p. 90   Pittman, L. D., & Richmond, A. (2007). Academic and psychological functioning in late adolescence: The importance of school belonging. *The Journal of Experimental Education, 75*(4), 270–290.

p. 92   The 50th Annual PDK Poll of the Public's Attitudes toward the Public Schools. Teaching: Great respect, dwindling appeal. (2018). Phi Delta Kappan, 100(1).

p. 94   Hart Research Associates. It takes more than a major and student success: employer priorities for college learning. (2013). Liberal Education, 99(2), 22.

p. 94   Caplan, M., Adams, J., & Michelene, T.H. (2018). *Work in progress: Dialogue videos foster interaction between homework partners.* 2018 ASEE Annual Conference & Exposition. Salt Lake City, Utah.

9

Lessons on Overcoming

I walked into a tall building on the south side of Tampa and up a flight of stairs to find Jen's office. I'd met Jennifer Samuel-Chance through the National Speakers Association when she did a presentation for our aspiring speakers group. From the minute she opened her mouth, I was mesmerized. Jen came from London by way of Trinidad, so her accent is quite unique. She also speaks with a deep, almost baritone resonance. If velvet had a sound, it would be Jen's voice. During her presentation, I sat in awe of the way she instantly commanded the room and held each of us captive for hours with her stories. I thought if I could just learn to be more like Jen, this TEDx talk would be a breeze.

Of course, Jen immediately corrected me. I couldn't learn to be Jen. We have very different voices and personalities. Even if I could learn to imitate her well, it would seem inauthentic to the audience. Instead, we would work together to identify my strengths and make me the best speaker I could be. Jen's guidance reminded me of the advice I give to interns who try to imitate the experienced teachers they admire: their students never respond as well as when the young teachers find their own authentic teacher personas. This wouldn't be the only connection between Jen's speaking advice and effective teaching practices.

After a series of exercises, Jen sent me home with a task: learn my talk so well that I didn't need to think about what sentence came next. I was to walk around the block repeating my talk and listen to it before going to sleep each night. My goal was to

DOI: 10.4324/9781003122029-10

know it in my bones so that I could focus on the emotion and respond to the audiences' emotions. Again, I made a connection to teaching. When I was a novice teacher first beginning to teach lessons, I was so focused on my lesson plans and next moves that I hardly noticed the students in front of me. After months of teaching, I began to use the lesson plan as a guide and freely make adjustments in response to the students.

Experienced teachers do this naturally. They know the bliss of being fully engaged in a lesson with their students, what is often called being "in the zone." They live for those rare and wonderful moments when the bell surprises both student and teacher because everyone has lost track of time. Psychologist Mihaly Csikszentmihalyi calls this *flow*. In a state of flow, we employ our highest strengths to meet our highest challenges. We become completely absorbed in a difficult but doable task. It's tempting to think we'd be happier if we avoided challenges and stayed in a comfortable, safe space. But according to Dr. Csikszentmihalyi, the best moments are not those when we are passive and relaxed; the best moments occur when we are stretched to our limits in a voluntary effort to accomplish something worthwhile.

Dr. Csikszentmihalyi describes flow as a state in which people become so absorbed in activity that nothing else seems to matter. Flow is such a rewarding state that people will work to get there, even at great cost. The hours we've spent developing our skills enable us to reach this state. Being in flow requires preparation and being fully present, and it is most likely to happen when we are working with others. The response between teacher and learner, or the response between speaker and audience, certainly enhances this state. I have often experienced flow as a teacher, and I longed to experience it as a speaker. But, as Jen reminded me, first I'd have to put in the hours.

Overcoming Trauma

After months of preparation, I embarked on the two-hour drive from Lakeland to Eustis for the TEDxEustis dress rehearsal. I pulled into the parking lot just as the sun was coming up and shining a golden glow on the Old Bay State Theatre. The theater opened as a vaudeville house in 1922 and had been beautifully renovated. Once inside, I stopped for a few minutes to take in its charm. I looked over the 500 seats and made my way to a row near the front where the speakers were seated. We were welcomed by Tim Totten and his co-organizer, Byron Faudie. I was happy to hear the familiar voice of curator Peter Kenjosian, who had been checking in with me regularly with regard to my progress. Peter instructed us to come up on the stage when called and give our talk just as we would during tomorrow's event. We would go in the order listed on the program. I was last, so I settled in to watch my fellow speakers.

One of the first to take the stage was Lea Tran, a petite brunette with an infectious smile. Her talk was riveting. Lea comes from a family of Chinese descent who experienced oppression after the fall of Saigon in 1975. At the age of 16, Lea, along with her parents and siblings, fled Vietnam for a better life. Their journey was arduous. Lea was separated from her parents when they boarded the boat. In her talk she described the crowded, unsanitary conditions on the lower deck where she stayed, huddled with strangers. In the middle of the sea, the boat was overtaken by pirates, and the passengers were robbed of their possessions and supplies. They were adrift at sea for days before being rescued by an oil rig. Lea and her family were eventually sent to a refugee camp in Indonesia. After recovering from malaria, the family was finally on their way to begin a new life in the United States—Minnesota to be exact.

Lea described the difficulty of assimilating to a new culture and learning a new language as a young person. While struggling to adjust, she was also still trying to overcome the traumatic events she had experienced. Trauma can impede a person's ability to learn, to form positive relationships, and to regulate emotions. A sense of hopelessness, lack of control, and distrust also often accompany trauma. There can be lasting, detrimental effects, particularly on children. Educational researcher Patricia Jennings has studied what teachers can do to support students experiencing trauma.

Dr. Jennings suggests that positive school experiences can mitigate the detrimental impact of trauma, particularly when schools provide a predictable and safe environment. She recommends that educators focus on developing secure attachments with students who have experienced trauma. The more reliable and predictable teacher behaviors are, the more trust can be developed between student and teacher. In addition, teachers can help students learn to recognize escalating emotions and practice calming strategies. Most importantly, Dr. Jennings advises teachers to resist questions like, *What's wrong with this student?* Instead, it can be more helpful to ask, *What happened to this student and how did the student learn to adapt to it?* Understanding a student's story is essential to helping the student overcome the impact of trauma. I wondered how many of Lea's teachers knew about her distressing journey.

After Lea rehearsed, we had the opportunity to talk. We discussed her school experiences and the many teachers who had helped her. Lea mentioned one professor who taught a lesson that stuck with her. After graduating from high school, she attended Villanova University to major in organic chemistry. Dr. Ludwig was one of her first chemistry professors. Lea remembers him sharing that he calculated the cost per minute of the students' time in his class. "It cost us twenty-five cents per minute to be there," Lea revealed. "As an immigrant, I understood the value of a quarter. So, I decided to make the most of my time. I studied hard and asked questions. I began taking the maximum number of courses I could for my tuition." Lea explained how the practice of calculating the value of her time continued to impact her life. She became determined to never waste a minute.

Lea's story made me think of the many challenges facing our immigrant students, those who have overcome countless obstacles in pursuit of a better life. Many of them are trying to assimilate while overcoming the traumatic events they experienced in their home countries and on their journeys. But like Lea, they tend to be hard-working and determined to make the most of every opportunity. I was in awe of Lea's courage and her resilience. I treasure the note she wrote in my TEDxEustis program: "Keep doing brave things. Don't miss the boat to the life of your dreams."

Overcoming Injustice

I was certain the speakers couldn't get any better, but then Fred Jones took to the stage. He was a commanding presence in his sheriff uniform and, if I closed my eyes, he sounded just like actor Samuel L. Jackson. Fred began with a roleplay depicting a traffic stop that suddenly escalated into the use of force. Then he posed some thought provoking questions: *What if a simple encounter between a law enforcement officer and a citizen doesn't need to become a confrontation? What if there is an alternative?* The key, Fred explained, is training that increases officers' emotional, social, and racial intelligence. This training had been helping the officers who participated understand themselves and how their own emotional states impact the way they interact with others.

One of the most powerful parts of Fred's talk was the story of 17-year-old Fred Jones out training for a cross-country event. He was on mile six of an eight-mile run when he was surrounded by police cars. Apparently, Fred fit the description of a suspect who had broken into a nearby house. He was quickly put into the back seat and driven to the crime scene. Fortunately, the home-owner said he was not the same young man who had broken in. Before he knew it, Fred was back in the car and quickly dropped off at the place where the officers stopped him. They sped away without saying a word.

Fred was angry. He avoided any contact with law enforce-ment officers for a long time—until he decided to become one. He wondered out loud how his experience may have been different if the officers had been more emotionally, socially, and racially intelligent. Would the encounter have made a different kind of impact on his life? As a Black man and an officer, Fred has encountered negative stereotypes from all sides. And so, he advocates for the compassionate treatment of all people as individuals.

Fred's retelling of his encounter with law enforcement made me think about the disparities that exist for Black males in schools. Around the same time Fred was in high school, educational researcher and advocate Gloria Ladson-Billings began studying the educational experiences and outcomes of Black male students. Measures of achievement and graduation rates tend to be much lower for this group than others. They are also much more likely to face disciplinary consequences and be excluded from school for disciplinary reasons. These disparities impact their economic futures and the quality of their lives. Low expectations and stereotypes have led to inequitable opportunities for Black male students for decades.

Dr. Ladson-Billings identified teaching practices that lead to better outcomes for Black male students. She recommends teachers start with the question, *What does this student need to be more fully engaged in the classroom community?* Often, the answer to this question lies in a classroom culture of high expectations as well as a sense of community and belonging. Culturally relevant teaching is another critical component. Students need to see themselves and their communities represented in the curriculum. Effective teachers also identify their students' cultural strengths and build upon them.

When Fred's rehearsal ended, I had a chance to talk with him. I asked about how he got over the anger following his encounter with law enforcement. It turns out, a teacher played a role in his healing. Mr. Dammervile was Fred's high school English teacher and cross-country coach. Fred was in a remedial English class, even though he liked to read and write. "I just didn't see myself as academically capable, and I was in the class with my friends," he said. "One day, Mr. Dammervile kept me after class. He told me I wasn't living up to my potential. He challenged me to do better." Fred shared that Mr. Dammervile began to assign him books by Black authors, like Alice Walker, Maya Angelou, and James Baldwin. He wanted Fred to see examples of scholars and writers who looked like him.

"I returned to school that Monday after my encounter with the officers," Fred continued. "Mr. Dammervile could see I was distraught. I told him what happened and how angry I felt."

Fred then described the way his teacher helped him talk about his emotions and find ways to release them, and he reassured Fred that not all officers are like that. "Mr. Dammervile went out of his way to show me that race doesn't have to be a barrier in relationships, that we can all learn to respect and appreciate each other." It occurred to me that Fred now teaches others what Mr. Dammervile taught him. I thought about Mr. Dammervile's high expectations and provision of role models. I could clearly identify aspects of Dr. Ladson-Billings' research in Fred's description of his teacher.

I mentioned to Fred that teachers could use the same kind of training in emotional, social, and racial intelligence that law enforcement officers were receiving. I explained that incidents in the classroom can be escalated or calmed by a teacher's response. Fred agreed, and he then introduced me to his wife, Dana, an educator who had used many of the strategies she learned from Fred with her own students. The three of us talked about the opportunity of those in a position of power to impact lives, either positively or negatively. We all acknowledged one truth: the kind of impact we make is largely determined by the way we govern ourselves.

Overcoming Failure

After a full day of rehearsing, the TEDxEustis speakers were invited to a dinner. I was seated next to Holly, the daughter of one of the speakers. Holly was a recent college graduate who had moved to California to pursue a career in acting. I asked her about the challenge of persisting through the audition process, which seemed to be fraught with rejection. Holly described her habit of framing failures as feedback. She tried to stay engaged in the process, to continually improve, rather than focusing solely on the outcome. And, it turns out, there was a teacher who helped her develop this mindset. Holly told me about Miss Neal, her second grade teacher, who helped her recognize the necessity of struggle in growth.

Holly described a big oak tree in the middle of the playground at her elementary school. Every fall, the ground underneath the tree would be covered in acorns. Holly and her friends would collect the prettiest ones and bring them to their teacher, Miss Neal. "Our teacher patiently admired each one," Holly remembered. "She would hold them up and tell us that all the makings of a big tree were hidden in a tiny acorn. Miss Neal also explained that the acorns would have to go through some tough times before becoming trees. Some would get buried by squirrels and forgotten. Some would get buried under leaves and sticks and stay there through the winter."

Then Holly shared what impacted her most from Miss Neal's lesson. "She told us that we were like acorns. We each had the potential to do big, amazing things. We would go through challenges, but those challenges would help us grow strong. I never forgot Miss Neal's words. I even keep a jar of acorns on my desk to remind me of my strength and potential."

I told Holly that her story reminded me of the research of Stanford psychologist Carol Dweck, whose work contrasts the outcomes of a fixed mindset versus a growth mindset. A person using a fixed mindset assumes that character, intelligence, and abilities are static and can't be changed, while a person using a growth mindset sees possibilities for improvement with time and effort. The mindset a person uses most consistently has a profound impact on success and satisfaction. Dr. Dweck found that using a fixed mindset leads to a focus on gaining approval and avoiding failure. Using a growth mindset leads to a focus on challenge and persistence. A growth mindset allows people to thrive, even during difficult times, which allows people to see failure as a vehicle for feedback and a springboard to improvement.

Holly immediately saw the connection between Carol Dweck's research and her beloved teacher's words. "Miss Neal taught me as much about life as she did about reading, math, or science. And so many other teachers built upon that foundation." That same sense of gratitude Holly felt for her teachers, I felt for my Coach Jen. She knew that we had to start with my mindset and beliefs. We practiced visualization and affirmations before we tackled my talk. Somehow Jen knew I first had to believe in the possibility of improvement. I had to see it before I could be it.

Overcoming Fear

When the morning of the TEDxEustis event finally arrived, I felt nervous but ready. Brian was attending a conference, so I had come to Eustis on my own. As I walked up to the theater, I was surprised by two enthusiastic supporters: Cailin and Jake were wearing matching t-shirts with the logo we had created for the Chalk and Chances website. They were practically bouncing with excitement. The two of them were ready to experience everything that a TEDx event had to offer.

We found seats in the middle of the theater just as Tim came on stage to introduce the first speaker. I watched as Cailin cried through Lea's talk and Jake led a standing ovation after Fred's. During the lunch break, they eagerly conversed with all of the speakers in the room.

After lunch, I headed backstage to prepare for my talk. Kathy, the stage manager, carefully tucked my microphone cord behind my collar while speaking words of encouragement. Before going on, I closed my eyes and worked my way through the relaxation techniques Jen had prescribed. She was adamant that any anxiety I brought onto the stage would be picked up by the audience. "Emotions and energy are contagious," Jen would say. I knew she was right because I had seen that phenomenon occur in classrooms over and over again. So, I thought about what I wanted the audience members to feel, and I focused on the kind of experience I wanted them to have.

As I walked onto the stage, I was blinded by the spotlights, but I could see my two supporters in the front row. My nerves quickly disappeared, and I became fully engaged in delivering a message about the ways teachers can change students' hearts, minds, and lives. I told the audience how Miss Andrews helped John feel worthy through her gift of the shirts. I talked about the way Mr. Mann helped Jay feel competent by focusing on one lesson at a time. And I relayed the ways we could all support teachers better. Then I left the audience with a challenge, to honor their teachers by intentionally making an impact on the people they encounter. The 17 minutes went by quickly, and I managed to share my message without any major snafus. Since my talk was the last, I was soon joined on stage by all of my fellow speakers and the TEDxEustis team. Going through the experience together had bonded us in a way that I didn't anticipate.

The TEDx experience further validated Mihaly Csikszentmihalyi's research for me. It was much more satisfying to have stretched myself in the service of something worthwhile than to have remained in a place of familiarity and comfort. Our students find this same fulfilment in being stretched. Whether they have experienced trauma, discrimination, or past failures, they need us to hold high expectations for their success. All of our students have something to overcome, and some of our students have much to overcome. They don't need us to save them. They need us to create the conditions in which they can propel themselves toward their potential.

I couldn't bask in the satisfying afterglow of TEDxEustis for too long. Soon, I'd be heading to a conference for educators, and I couldn't wait to share my research with them. It was another opportunity to practice the skills Jen taught me. I would carry everything I learned from TEDxEustis just as I continued to carry what I learned from the craft fair, the farmers' market, and the university campus. With each story, I knew a little more about the kinds of classrooms in which students thrive. When we create classrooms where our students feel safe, seen, and stretched, the acorns in our care can eventually become magnificent oaks.

Applying Lessons on Overcoming

Our students' lives outside of school impact the ways they act and interact in our classrooms. Often, behaviors that hinder their progress are just defenses or coping mechanisms they have developed in response to events in their lives. The environment in our classrooms can be a mitigating factor for students who are overcoming significant challenges. Below are three areas of focus for helping students overcome challenges and reach their potential.

Area 1: Overcoming Trauma

Students who have experienced a traumatic event or who have experienced adverse conditions over time need a school environment that feels safe and predictable. They need teachers who are reliable and benevolent.

How can you intentionally create a safe, predictable, and accepting classroom culture?

Seemingly small incidents may trigger a fight, flight, or freeze response, but teachers and other school personnel can help students recognize escalating emotions and practice calming strategies.

How can you recognize the signs of distress in your students and help them recognize these signs in themselves? What strategies could you incorporate to help your students return to a state of calm?

Area 2: Overcoming Injustice

Low expectations, stereotypes, and inequitable opportunities have long impacted students of color. Better outcomes require teachers who hold high expectations and who help students hold high expectations for themselves.

What kind of expectations do your actions and interactions in the classroom convey? What is the level of challenge and relevancy in the instruction you are providing to your students of color?

Honoring and respecting students' home cultures and providing representations of their cultures in the classroom helps students feel a sense of belonging in the academic community.

How are you incorporating culturally relevant resources into your instruction? How do your students of color see their home cultures honored in your classroom?

Area 3: Overcoming Failure

The way in which students view failure impacts their effort and perseverance. Viewing failure as a reflection of their unchangeable ability may keep them from attempting or persisting through a difficult task. Viewing failure as an opportunity for feedback and improvement is a more empowering stance.

How can you evaluate students' progress (and help them evaluate their own progress) as a path to growth rather than a judgment of their ability?

How can you use mistakes and incorrect answers as tools for increased understanding?

Notes and Works Cited

p. 99   Csikszentmihalyi, M. (2008). *Flow : the psychology of optimal experience.* Harper Perennial Modern Classics.

p. 100   YouTube. (2019). *I did not miss the boat | Lea Tran | TEDxEustis.* YouTube. https://www.youtube.com/watch?v=z9kPGAZ-hGQ.

p. 100   Tran, L. (2020). *I did not miss the boat: memoir of a Vietnam Hoa refugee.* Suncoast Digital Press.

p. 101   Jennings, P. A., & Siegel, D. J. (2019). *The trauma-sensitive classroom : building resilience with compassionate teaching.* W.W. Norton & Company.

p. 102   YouTube. (2019). *Use of voice not force | Fred Jones | TEDxEustis.* YouTube. https://www.youtube.com/watch?v=4tCJPEili80.

p. 103   Ladson-Billings, G. (2009). *The dreamkeepers.: Successful teachers of African American children. (2nd ed.).* Jossey-Bass.

p. 105   Dweck, C. S. (2006). *Mindset: the new psychology of success.* Random House.

p. 106   YouTube. (2019). *The teachers we remember | Julie Hasson | TEDxEustis.* YouTube. https://www.youtube.com/watch?v=nmwy6r26vQY.

10

Lessons on Equity

Feeling a bit apprehensive, I put my suitcase in the car and headed to Tampa International Airport. Flying is fraught with possibilities for frustration, from delays to gate changes to lost luggage. I always carry books and other reading material to distract myself. On the plane from Tampa to Philadelphia, I selected the sessions I wanted to attend at the National Association of Professional Development Schools annual conference. The focus of the conference was equity, an examination of how we can provide the resources and support needed for all students to reach their full potential. Conference sessions emphasized setting goals and expectations equally high for all students with the understanding that the support needed to achieve those goals may differ. I spent the rest of the flight and the ride from Philadelphia to Atlantic City pondering one question: Why are the educational systems in our nation still struggling to provide equitable opportunities for students? I thought about the Kerner Report, released over 50 years ago, which highlighted racial division and disparities in the United States. The Kerner Report served as a call to action in 1968, and over the next decade efforts directed at desegregation, school finance reform, and increased investment in underprivileged communities started to level the playing field. However, the gains made during the 1970s began to diminish in the 1980s when federal programs supporting educational opportunities in impoverished urban and rural areas were reduced or eliminated.

DOI: 10.4324/9781003122029-11

Despite more recent legislation intended to close achievement gaps, disparities continue. According to Linda Darling-Hammond, educational researcher and President of the Learning Policy Institute, the years from 2002 until 2015 (the era of No Child Left Behind) were characterized by investments in testing without investing in the resources needed to help all students achieve higher standards. In addition to the ongoing redirection of needed resources to testing, resegregation into separate and unequal schools has continued to increase in many parts of the United States. Dr. Darling-Hammond warns that no society can thrive in a technological, knowledge-based economy by depriving large segments of its population of the resources and opportunities needed for learning. In many ways, the future hinges on our efforts to create a more equitable educational system.

Continuous Reflection

I spent the first day of the conference attending presentations and panel discussions related to the ways in which power imbalances and cultural differences impact students. As a woman who identifies as White and middle class, my culture is predominant in academics. Therefore, I find myself continuously reflecting on the ways my background and perspective shape my teaching and my research. I know that I make inaccurate assumptions about other people, often without consciously doing so. We all do. One way to uncover our unconscious biases is to reflect on how our beliefs manifest in the classroom. Who do we call upon to take leadership roles? Who participates most in class discussions? Who receives more praise or feedback? Unconscious biases are not easily eradicated, but if we become aware of them, they need not drive our behavior.

Researcher, author, and activist Lisa Delpit has studied the ways classroom interactions are often laden with assumptions about the capabilities, motivations, and values of students of color. Some students' academic struggles are the result of miscommunication or misunderstandings. Teachers may use

language, styles of instruction, or discipline practices that are
out of alignment with the norms of a student's community. We
cannot hope to connect with the students in front of us if we
don't understand their families and communities. Students can
feel invisible in classrooms where their cultures are not understood or where their differences are seen as deficits.

Many of the presentations I attended carried the same
message as Dr. Delpit's books: failing to acknowledge that there
are multiple, valid worldviews creates power imbalances and
cultural conflicts in classrooms. If educators are to improve academic outcomes for all students, we must work to overcome the
power differential, stereotypes, and other barriers that prevent
us from seeing and appreciating all students. If our goal is to
educate all students well, we have to examine our own blind
spots and attempt to truly and justly see the students we teach.

Opportunity Gaps

I'd been invited to give the luncheon keynote on the second day
of the conference. By the time I finished my talk, I was famished.
As the participants left the ballroom, I finally sat down to eat my
lunch. Feeling awkward eating alone, I was happy to see Ray
approach and ask if he could join me. I recognized him from a
panel discussion on opportunity gaps I had attended. Ray was
seeking a doctoral degree in curriculum and instruction with a
focus on equity. He was also the chair of an equity committee in
the school district where he taught high school. I told him how
I'd been wondering about the intersection of my research with
equity work. Ray's answer was affirming. "Feeling safe, seen,
and stretched is good for all students, but for school-dependent
students, being in a classroom culture of safe, seen, and stretched
is critical." Ray defined school-dependent students as those who
need effective teachers in order to be academically successful and
who need the foundation schools provide to achieve an economically secure future. The parents of school-dependent students
may not have the skills, time, or resources to support them in the
way that economically stable families could.

Pedro Noguera, researcher and noted expert on educational equity, suggests that students arrive at school with different needs, and thus, need different levels of support in order to reach their full potential. According to Dr. Noguera, we will know that we are effectively addressing issues of equity when students' backgrounds no longer predict their outcomes. It's not just students' backgrounds that contribute to inequity, it's also the opportunities available to them. Not only do some students have greater resources at home, they also have greater access to advanced coursework, tutoring, and extracurricular activities at school. But just offering the same access to opportunities is not equity. Some students also need more support to succeed in those opportunities. Opportunities plus support equals equity.

Ray added to my understanding of Pedro Noguera's work by discussing educational practices that can impede equity, such as tracking and labeling. Then he told me about his own experience as a young student and the teacher who helped him find a new path.

"At the end of my third grade year, my mother was invited to a meeting to discuss testing me for a disability," he said. "I was struggling significantly in all subjects and a screening test suggested I might fit a diagnosis of Educable Mentally Handicapped."

Ray admitted he didn't understand what that meant at the time and his mother likely didn't either. Fortunately, he began his fourth grade year in the hands of Mrs. Simon. "After a couple of weeks, she called my mom. She asked her to wait on the testing and said she believed I just needed more time and individual attention." Ray recalls Mrs. Simon working with him one-on-one as often as she could, and even bringing books and workbooks to his house so that his older sister could help him after school.

Ray began to grow in competence and confidence. "Things started to click for me in Mrs. Simon's class. I began to see myself as a learner, and I figured out how I learn best." The teachers he had prior to Mrs. Simon had good intentions, Ray said, and likely believed the diagnosis would lead to more help and interventions. However, he also expressed his gratitude for Mrs. Simon seeing him differently. "Somehow she knew this label would be a life sentence of low expectations for me, as it is for many students of color. Despite my past performance, she saw potential. She must have understood that living in poverty, frequently relocating, and dealing with a turbulent home life impacted my achievement. She must have sensed that my environment influenced my struggle, rather than my inherent ability." Sitting there with Ray, I suddenly felt grateful for his teacher, too. Because Mrs. Simon believed in his potential and invested in his success, he now makes a positive impact on the next generation of students.

My years as a teacher and principal had opened my eyes to the ambiguity and subjectivity that often accompany the process of identifying a disability. I was also aware of the overrepresentation of students of color and students living in poverty in programs serving students with exceptionalities. Researchers Beth Harry and Janette Klingner have identified several environmental factors that can contribute to lack of academic achievement, including poverty, unsafe conditions in the community, and lack of access to books. Economic instability itself is not the cause of learning difficulties, but it is often accompanied by lack of nutrition and lack of experiences, which may lead to delays in motor and language development. These environmental factors, as well as ineffective instruction in the early years, can easily be mistaken for a disability. Some students do have innate challenges that impact their physical and/or cognitive functioning, and they have a right to accommodations or modifications needed for learning. But I couldn't help wondering about ways to provide support and interventions while holding high expectations for all students.

Culturally Responsive Teaching

After my lunch conversation with Ray, I headed to the exhibit hall where the student research projects were displayed. The title on one poster caught my eye: *Using Culturally Responsive Instruction to Improve the Reading Achievement of English Language Learners*. The researcher, Ines, happened to be standing by the poster, ready for questions. I asked how she selected texts and how she assessed the students' growth. She explained her process and provided me with details about her results. Then she told me the project was inspired by a professor who introduced her to Geneva Gay's research. Dr. Gay is an award-winning professor and researcher known for her scholarship in multicultural education. Her writings reflect the promise of culturally responsive teaching as a path to greater equity.

According to Dr. Gay, discontinuity between a student's community culture and school culture can be a factor in achievement. Reading, writing, and language are the foundations of academics, and culture is infused in the ways students think, write, and speak. Therefore, aligning instruction to a student's culture can significantly improve learning. Culturally responsive teaching entails using students' cultural knowledge, prior experiences, and frames of reference to make learning tasks more relevant. Matching classroom structures and environments to the cultural experiences of the learner can also increase engagement. Culturally responsive teaching helps students feel seen.

Students also feel seen when people like them are represented in their classrooms and schools. Decorations and materials featuring people of different races, religions, countries, ages, abilities, and family structures indicate an inclusive environment. A culturally diverse collection of books and materials also sends a message to students about the value of diverse cultures. The presence of diversity in the classroom allows students to consider perspectives and opinions beyond those already familiar to them through family and friends. Exposing students to different perspectives gives them the opportunity to think critically about their own beliefs and examine the world in new ways.

After we talked about Geneva Gay's impact on our teaching philosophies, Ines shared a story about one of her own teachers who recognized and valued cultural diversity. "My family moved from Portugal to California when I was eight," she began. "My English was limited, and I felt self-conscious when I tried to speak. I was so nervous about starting third grade at my new neighborhood school." Ines worried the other students would make fun of her language and her accent. But when she walked into the classroom on the first day, she was greeted by Miss Wilcox.

"She had the most beautiful smile. She took my hand, and to my surprise, she greeted me in Portuguese. While I had been trying to learn English, my teacher had been trying to learn my home language. It made me feel so special." Ines described the ways Miss Wilcox helped her learn English, and she helped her teacher learn Portuguese. The other kids noticed and wanted to learn too.

Miss Wilcox celebrated Ines' culture, and even invited her mother to class to talk about life in Portugal. "Instead of feeling uncomfortable about being different or ashamed of my native language, Miss Wilcox helped me feel proud." Because she was curious about Ines' culture and wanted to learn her language, the other students felt inspired to approach Ines with curiosity rather than judgment. "I am so grateful to Miss Wilcox for embracing me and helping me feel at home," she said.

Ines and I agreed that culturally responsive teaching doesn't just improve academic performance, it improves social and emotional outcomes as well. Dr. Gay defines caring in culturally responsive teaching as a combination of warmth and challenge. Caring teachers honor the humanity of all students, regard them with high esteem, and expect high performance from them. They view students' challenges with concern and compassion while continuing to invest in their success. By seeing, respecting, and supporting students in a culturally responsive way, teachers foster self-confidence and self-reliance. These teachers empower their students as they focus on their strengths rather than viewing differences as deficits. In culturally responsive teaching, helping students feel safe and seen is not enough—feeling stretched is also critical.

Expectations and Efficacy

When the conference ended, I returned to the terminal in the Philadelphia Airport with a notebook full of ideas. The conference had been packed with thought-provoking presentations and conversations. Luckily, I spotted one open seat near the gate where I could organize my notes while waiting for my turn to board the plane. As I sat down and pushed my bags under the seat, I noticed a logo on the back pack of the young woman next to me. I looked over and asked her, "Do you attend the University of Central Florida?" She responded by telling me that she is in her second year there and is majoring in engineering. I told her about my son, Connor, who graduated from UCF two years earlier with an engineering degree. We talked about the professors they both had and their experiences in the program. Then I closed my notebook and listened intently as my new friend, Maria, told me about her path to the university.

"I grew up in a migrant family," she said. "Most people don't understand what that's like, especially for a high school student. Our family moved three or four times a school year. Each time, I would lose credits because some courses didn't transfer. I would be ahead in some classes and behind in others. I felt like I could not compete for scholarships, and scholarships were my only hope for a better life."

Maria described one high school science teacher, Mr. Diaz, who had been a migrant student himself. He noticed her academic potential and encouraged her. "One day after school, he went to my home and explained to my family that I had a good chance for a scholarship if I could just stay put and finish high school at his school," she said. Mr. Diaz convinced Maria's parents to let her live with an aunt and uncle so she could focus on schoolwork. He made sure Maria had a ride when she stayed after school for STEM club. He even helped her with college essays and applications.

"Now I am a college sophomore and one of a handful of girls in my engineering class. I know that I have to work harder to prove myself because I am a migrant and a girl, but I am grateful to have this chance." Then Maria explained that she had a dream even bigger than becoming an engineer. "I want to do well so that I can do for other girls what Mr. Diaz did for me. My dream is to start a foundation to support migrant girls and help them go to college."

Maria's dream sounded like a perfect way to honor Mr. Diaz, and I spent the flight home thinking about how many girls like

Maria did not reach their potential because they didn't have someone like him. What made him so impactful? For one thing, he focused on what he could influence. He couldn't raise her family out of poverty, but he could assist Maria and advise her parents. Mr. Diaz had a high degree of professional efficacy—the belief that he could positively impact student outcomes. Educational researcher Patricia Ashton spent decades studying professional efficacy and how it influences a teacher's actions and interactions. In teaching, belief in our own competence inspires our behavior. Efficacy influences a teacher's instructional decisions, the degree of effort applied to teaching, and the willingness to persist in the face of challenges.

Teacher efficacy is also related to expectations. Teachers who feel a strong sense of self-confidence and efficacy in their teaching abilities have high expectations for their students' achievement. They choose challenging activities for their students because they believe they can guide and support them in those tasks. However, Dr. Ashton warns that efficacy can be situation-specific. Teachers may feel a high degree of efficacy in only certain subjects or with certain groups of learners. Ensuring equity in education requires building a high degree of efficacy for teaching all students, especially those who are school-dependent. For better or worse, students internalize their teachers' expectations and perform accordingly. Our students will rise to the level of our beliefs—about them and about ourselves.

The Lens of Curiosity

When I think about cultural knowledge and responsiveness, I remember the warning of my former sociology professor, Dr. Plowman. He would remind me to keep in mind the variability of individuals within cultures. Culture intersects with gender, economic status, and personality, making everyone's experience unique. Because of this, the most productive stance may be one of curiosity. Dr. Plowman always advocated for asking questions rather than making assumptions. I considered the questions a curious teacher might ask about each student, particularly those with different backgrounds than their teacher. What is this student's experience like in our classroom? What has happened in this student's life, and how has the student adapted? What are this student's strengths and how can I build upon them? What does this student need to be fully engaged in the classroom community?

The questions felt empowering, and I decided to add them to my notes for school visits in the coming weeks. My presentations at conferences had led to invitations to present my research at schools and in school districts. It was perfect timing because I had become curious about the influence of school and district cultures on teachers' abilities to be responsive in their classrooms. I wondered how high-stakes accountability systems were impacting the ways teachers made their students feel safe, seen, and stretched. The conversations I'd had with principals in scheduling school presentations revealed a disconnect. Many didn't understand how strengthening relationships could increase achievement. I also began to wonder if the administrators who had invited me to speak understood the importance of helping their teachers feel safe, seen, and stretched. Schools can't become the best places for students to learn and grow unless we also make them the best places for teachers to work and grow. I wondered how teachers were coping with the competing priorities of test preparation and responding to students' individual needs. I wouldn't have to wonder for too long.

Applying Lessons on Equity

Equity requires that we hold high expectations for all students while providing the support each student needs to reach those expectations. Understanding our students' cultures and the way culture impacts learning is a step in the direction of more equitable outcomes. Our (often unconscious) beliefs influence the ways we act and interact with students. Below are three areas of focus for ensuring all students feel safe, seen, and stretched in our classrooms.

Area 1: Unconscious Biases

Everyone makes assumptions; it's human nature to make quick judgments about others. Identifying our biases is key in keeping them from disempowering students. There are assessments to help in identifying biases, such as The Implicit Association Test, which explores associations based on race, gender, religion, and other characteristics. Reflecting on your decisions and actions may also reveal unconscious biases.

Consider who participates most in class discussions.

Consider whether the examples you use in class are counter-stereotypical.

Reflect on the expectations you have of students from different cultures, and consider how your expectations are demonstrated in the classroom.

Area 2: Opportunity Gaps

A number of factors contribute to success for all children. These include a high-quality core instructional program, ongoing assessment, and appropriate interventions and supports to meet each student's needs. Some students come to school with the benefit of resources and support at home, and these students often also have the advantage of access to advanced coursework, tutoring, and extracurricular activities at school. Ensuring equity of opportunities requires examining schoolwide data and practices.

Consider any disproportionate representation in programs. Are some groups overly represented (compared to the overall school population) in enrichment or remedial programs?

Consider how data and evidence are used (rather than subjective opinions) in decision making regarding selection for programs.

Consider how families are kept informed (in their home languages) about options for their students.

Area 3: Culturally Responsive Teaching

Culturally responsive teaching entails using students' cultural knowledge, prior experiences, and frames of reference to make learning tasks more relevant. Teachers who are responsive to students' cultures seek information from families and communities to inform their practice. Being culturally responsive requires reflecting on different aspects of culture and instruction.

Consider how your communication in the classroom aligns with students' communication in their communities.

Consider how students' cultures influence their participation styles in the classroom.

Consider how students' experiences and frames of reference influence their ability to understand concepts.

Notes and Works Cited

p. 110   Goodsen, S.T. & Myers, S.L. (2018). The Kerner Commission Report fifty years later: Revisiting the American dream. *The Russell Sage Foundation Journal of the Social Sciences, 4*(6), 1–17.

p. 111   Darling-Hammond, L. (2018, April 11). Kerner at 50: Educational equity still a dream deferred. *Learning Policy Institute*. https://learningpolicyinstitute.org/blog/kerner-50-educational-equity-still-dream-deferred.

p. 111   Delpit, L. (2006). *Other people's children : cultural conflict in the classroom*. New Press.

p. 113   Blankstein, A. M., Noguera, P., Kelly, L. (2016). *Excellence through equity: Five principles of courageous leadership to guide achievement for every student*. ASCD.

p. 114   Harry, B., & Klingner, J. (2007). Discarding the deficit model. *Educational Leadership, 5*, 16.

p. 115   Gay, G. (2018). *Culturally responsive teaching : theory, research, and practice (Third ed.)*. Teachers College Press.

p. 118   Ashton, P. T. (1984). Teacher efficacy: A motivational paradigm for effective teacher education. *Journal of Teacher Education, 35*, 28–32.

11

Lessons on Generativity

I pulled up to Greenhills Middle School just as the sun appeared over the east side of the main building. It reminded me of my own junior high with its flat-roofed buildings, painted beige and connected by covered hallways. Jenae Cook, the assistant principal, was waiting out front. Jenae and I met at a conference where she heard me speak about my research. She asked the principal, Michael Ashcroft, to invite me to lead their spring professional development day. It took some convincing before Mr. Ashcroft agreed. He was looking for an expedient way to boost test scores, and my offering was not a quick fix. On a call with the principal, I explained how strengthening student–teacher relationships could increase student achievement. Stronger relationships could also lead to less conflict and better emotional regulation. In other words, there may be less discipline issues to handle. I had him at "fewer students in your office."

Jenae led me to the auditorium, where she plugged my laptop into the projector and checked the microphone. She adjusted the focus and worried the slides wouldn't be sharp enough. I assured her that my slides had very little text and that our day would be much more conversation than presentation. Mr. Ashcroft's administrative assistant set up donuts and coffee in the back. I put my phone near the microphone and started my playlist (a mix of seventies folk rock) just as teachers began coming into the room. I've worked with teachers long enough to know that on a day with no students they are itching to catch up on grading and

DOI: 10.4324/9781003122029-12

planning. I hoped my music and the coffee would help soothe the itch.

Teachers typically walk into a professional development session the same way students walk into a classroom on the first day of school, sizing up the situation. They greet me warmly, but I can tell they are wondering if I'm competent and credible, if they will enjoy the day, and if they will learn something relevant that will help them grow. Most importantly, they are wondering if they will get to sit with their friends. Knowing this, I try to address those concerns as soon as possible. Jenae has talked me up, which helps. In speaking, like teaching, reputation can make your start with a new group a bit easier. Handouts were already at seats, with a clear agenda, goals for the day, and a brief bio so that we could start right away without an awkward introduction.

Passing the Torch

I started by talking about Mrs. Russell and the things she said and did to make a lasting impact on my life. I then asked the participants to think about the teachers who influenced their lives. After a few minutes to reflect and talk with a partner, I brought the group back together. One young woman, Jessica, raised her hand and asked to share.

"I had a tough childhood," she began. "I was taken from my mother and placed into foster care when I was 11. My sixth grade language arts teacher, Mrs. Dodd, knew what was going on and checked in with me every day. She did many of the things a mother would do, like making sure I signed up for tutoring and turned in the paperwork for field trips. She continued to support me even when I went on to high school. When I struggled, she attended conference night with me and talked to my teachers. She was a regular at my track meets. And I remember hearing her cheering when I walked across the stage at graduation."

Remembering our teachers always elicits emotions, but this group responded more dramatically to Jessica's story than I expected. I noticed tears throughout the room, and the woman next to Jessica was crying even harder than the rest. "I don't know what would have happened to me without Mrs. Dodd," Jessica continued. "She's the reason I became a teacher." Then she motioned for her crying colleague to stand, put her hand on the woman's shoulder, and spoke directly to me, "This is Mrs. Dodd."

Applause filled the auditorium. I asked Mrs. Dodd if she wanted to say something. She shook her head, unable to speak. Everyone in the room sat up a bit taller after that. Jessica's story hadn't just elevated Mrs. Dodd, it validated the importance of every teacher there. I'm certain their colleagues had known about their past connection, but they had probably never heard the full story. I suspected that many of them had become teachers because they, too, had a teacher like Mrs. Dodd. My friend, Daryl Ward, calls this phenomenon "generativity". Generativity occurs because of a desire to impact the next generation and also a desire to live on in their hearts and minds.

Daryl's dissertation research focused on a veteran humanities teacher who inspired countless students to become educators, many of whom became leaders in the district where she taught. This teacher's relationships with students transcended time and space. Daryl was intrigued by the notion that something in the teacher–student relationship could elicit a desire to replicate the experience for the next generation of students. Through interviews with this veteran teacher and her former students, Daryl realized that they didn't just inhabit her profession, they had internalized her teaching philosophy, pedagogical skills, and high expectations. Daryl's research was supported by Jessica's story and by countless other stories shared that day.

It was an engaging day digging into the concepts of safe, seen, and stretched. We considered models, shared examples, reflected, dissected, and dialogued until our heads and hearts were full. We wrapped up our day of professional development by each identifying one strategy we would commit to implementing over the next semester. The teachers chose accountability partners to help them stay on track. According to habits guru Charles Duhigg, change is more likely to stick if we start small and build in accountability and support. Information alone never leads to transformation. It must be consistently applied.

Fighting for Freedom

After I answered the questions and listened to the stories of the teachers who lingered, Jenae offered to give me a tour of the school. We started in one of my favorite spaces of any school: the art room. I always admire the brave and unfiltered self-expression of young artists. The gallery wall in this particular art room was full of sketches representing the Civil Rights Movement. The art teacher, Beth Dennis, explained how the sketches came from a collaborative project with the civics teachers. The students could depict a scene or a historical figure from the movement. I was impressed by the emotion conveyed in the sketches, such a beautiful combination of hope and pain. I asked Beth who or what inspired her to teach, and she told me about her middle school art teacher, Miss Akens.

"I took an art class as an elective in middle school. I wasn't good, but I loved the creative process," she said. "Halfway through the first semester, I felt like a failure. We were studying impressionism and the works of artists like Monet and Renoir. The other students were creating pieces with perfectly thin brushstrokes, while mine looked like it was dabbed with a big foam brush." Then she described the way her teacher encouraged her to look at her painting in a kinder and more generous way.

Miss Akens took Beth's painting and hung it on the other side of the classroom. She instructed her to stand back and look at it, telling her to squint and look through her eyelashes. She explained that some pieces are meant to be viewed that way.

"Miss Akens found something beautiful or interesting in every piece I created," Beth said. "She taught me that art is subjective and isn't supposed to be judged. Rather, it is supposed to express the soul of the artist and evoke emotion in the viewer." It was evident that Beth carried the same philosophy into her own classroom.

Then she shared a challenge that Miss Akens didn't experience: state policies requiring measures of impact for every teacher, including the art teacher. Her district created an assessment project for each art teacher to assign and a rubric by which to score the students' work. Beth confessed that using the rubric to score the emerging artists' work was contrary to her beliefs. The scores were being used to determine which teachers received performance pay, prompting some teachers to teach to the test. Beth shared her views on how these policies have undermined the willingness to take risks in the classroom for both students and teachers. Beth has made an effort to keep the test and the corresponding rubric from inhibiting creative expression in her classroom.

Author and education advocate Diane Ravitch writes about the consequences of policies that are based on business principles and developed without the input of educators. Policies focused on tying students' scores to teacher effectiveness fail to address the variables related to test scores that fall outside the influence of classrooms and schools. These policies also fail to recognize the inherent weaknesses in the tests themselves. Additionally, educators understand that student growth is cumulative. It's impossible to isolate achievement and growth from the students' experiences in prior years with prior teachers. Certainly well-prepared, well-qualified, committed teachers yield better results, but trying to measure teacher impact with test scores is an over-simplification at best. It also carries unintended consequences, like those that Beth was witnessing in her art classes.

Staying in the Fight

As Jenae and I walked down the social studies wing, a poster in one of the classrooms caught my eye. It featured a Muhammad Ali quote that my friend, Laura, also has displayed on her classroom wall: "I am the greatest. I said that even before I knew I was." Will Miller caught me peeking through his door and invited me in. I asked him about the Ali quote. Will told me it hangs in honor of his two inspirations, Muhammad Ali and his own social studies teacher, Mr. Porter.

"I grew up in a rough neighborhood just outside Chicago. Most of the kids didn't plan for the future. We were all just trying to get by," Will said. "My high school social studies teacher, Mr. Porter, grew up there, too. He left to become a professional boxer and came back to teach after he was injured. He also coached at the neighborhood boxing gym before and after school. In many ways he taught just like he coached his young boxers."

Will told me that before every test, Mr. Porter would remind the students that fighters never step in the ring without believing they're going to win. He made them talk about how they were going to dominate the test. "Mr. Porter always understood the power of beliefs. He taught us to speak words of confidence and to prepare so that we could back those words up."

Will described the day Mr. Porter asked him what he planned to do after high school. He admitted he wanted to go to college but didn't think he could get the scholarships he would need to pay for it. "Mr. Porter stopped me mid-sentence and made me talk about my goal in affirmations. He also helped me prepare for admissions tests and applications. I ended up with a full scholarship."

Will leaned back against his desk. "Now that I am a teacher and a coach, I try to speak greatness into my students, and I teach them to speak confidently about themselves. I am grateful to Mr. Porter for teaching me about the power of beliefs. I know he never got to fulfill his dreams as a boxer, but he helped countless students reach their dreams. I call that a success."

Mr. Porter was a beautiful example of generativity. Will did not just adopt his teacher's role; he also adopted his philosophy. Will shared another powerful practice that impacted his teaching: the practice of setting a daily intention. He realized that teaching, like boxing, requires goal-directed focus. And he was tired of letting forces outside his classroom determine his goals. Will felt overwhelmed by the amount of information coming at him all day. He began setting an intention as a proactive way to filter out what is unimportant and focus on what is most important. Will chose a specific intention—to reduce his students' suffering and increase their hope—and filtered through it each of the decisions he made in his classroom. Will also used the intention to judge his success. If, at the end of the day, he had increased his students' hope, that day was a win. The practice was empowering for Will and led to greater resilience and satisfaction in teaching.

Sustenance and Support

At the end of my tour with Jenae, I stopped to thank Mr. Ashcroft for the opportunity to work with his faculty. I sat in his office for a few minutes while he told me about the pressure he was under to increase test scores. The school had been threatened with a state takeover, in which all employees would have to reapply for their jobs. His fear, not just for himself but for his teachers, was driving his decisions. He asked for my advice, hoping for a quick fix. I gave him the same message I give all principals: "There are no shortcuts to better outcomes for students. No program or resource can match the time spent feeling safe, seen, and stretched in a great teacher's classroom," I told him. "Hire teachers who are passionate about students and passionate about teaching. Then support them, protect them, and grow them. That's it; that's the path to improvement. It's not quick, and it's not easy. And the path is made even more difficult by policies that hinder the ability of teachers to respond to students' needs."

Educational researchers Kerry Barnett and John McCormick investigated the influence of principal leadership on student learning outcomes. It is an indirect influence, moderated through the effectiveness of classroom instruction. But, according to these researchers, the quality of principals' relationships with individual teachers can strengthen teacher performance. One of a principal's chief responsibilities is the creation and communication of a compelling vision for school improvement and growth. Teachers are more likely to share that vision if they feel a principal knows them, understands their needs, and has their best interests at heart.

Demonstrating individual concern for teachers requires principals to be accessible, recognize individual efforts, and provide guidance. A principal who takes these actions shows commitment to the personal and professional well-being of teachers. As a result, those teachers are more likely to apply discretionary effort, try innovative teaching practices, and buy into the vision. Strong principal–teacher relationships contribute to a school culture in which *teachers* feel safe, seen, and stretched. For principals like Mr. Ashcroft, the bad news is that there are no hacks to building relationships, but the outcomes are worth the effort. The good news is, generativity is a phenomenon that applies to principals as well. Many teachers became school and district leaders because they were inspired by principals who invested in relationships with them.

Full Circle

I walked back into our bungalow with a long to-do list scrolling in my head. I was returning to the Lakeland Downtown Farmers' Market in the morning, and I needed to pack the car. Conferences and school visits had taken me away from data collection, and I was eager to gather more stories. Tucked away in the shed, my sign needed a dusting off. Luckily, my tote was right where I left it, still stocked with pens and notepads. As I rummaged through the kitchen cabinets for my refillable water bottle, the phone rang. I felt a lump in my throat when I saw Cailin's name. She had her first interview for a teaching position that afternoon. Brian, Jake, and I helped her prepare with practice questions. I'd texted words of encouragement in the morning, then tried to go on with my day as normal. It's funny how many times I'd interviewed prospective teachers as a principal but never gave a thought to their nervous moms.

Her voice had mixed tones of excitement and relief. "Mom, I got the job! I'm going to be teaching third grade." I told her how proud I was and reassured her that she was ready. I told her how much her great-grandmother, grandmother, and I had all loved teaching third grade. I listened as she shared her hopes and plans, but still I worried. Cailin had chosen to apply to an urban school in a neighborhood with great economic needs. On top of those challenges, in Florida, third grade is a mandatory retention year for students who don't meet proficiency standards in reading. The pressure on third grade reading teachers is undeniable. As a parent, I was concerned about that level of pressure on my novice teacher. However, I also knew she had the fortitude to navigate it. Like all great teachers, Cailin is a mixture of soft and strong. She has always been highly sensitive and empathetic, but she's always also been stubborn and tough.

I stopped my frenzied packing for a moment and sat down in the den to process Cailin's news. Teaching had changed since my years as a primary grades teacher—and maybe not for the better. The freedom to do projects or create units in response to current or seasonal events had been restricted by mandated curriculum calendars and highly scripted resources. Accountability legislation meant that she would be supervised closely by school and district leaders. Performance pay legislation might make her colleagues less likely to help her. I knew she loved kids and loved teaching, and I hoped that love would sustain her.

Just then the last rays of the day's sunlight shone through the glass apple on my desk, the one that was given to me by my mother. I found some tissue and a box, and I carefully packed the apple. I tucked a short note inside.

Dear Cailin,

I know you will make a big impact on your students and on our profession. It won't be easy, but it will be worth it.

Love, Mom

And so it goes, another generation of teachers begins the journey, inspired by the teachers who helped them feel safe, seen, and stretched.

I could've spent the rest of the evening pulling out Cailin's baby pictures and wondering where the time had gone, but I still had much to accomplish in preparation for the morning. I had a good feeling about what my second visit to the Lakeland Downtown Farmers' Market might hold.

Applying Lessons on Generativity

One of our professional charges is to replace ourselves with the next generation of teachers. When we are intentional in our work and model passion and purpose, we inspire our students to consider their own professional aspirations. And, if we are very lucky, our students become our colleagues. Below are three areas of reflection related to influence and intention.

Area 1: Influencing the Next Generation

Developing strong relationships has intrinsic value for both teachers and students, but those relationships may also create continuity between generations of teachers. Few things are more affirming for a teacher than a student expressing a desire to teach. These students typically enjoy learning, enjoy being in the classroom, and admire their teachers. They are also likely watching their teachers even more closely than other students.

What are your words and actions communicating to students about your profession?

How can you help aspiring teachers understand the challenges of the role without diminishing their excitement?

What teaching philosophies and pedagogical practices do you want your students to adopt from you?

Area 2: Setting an Intention

Setting a daily intention is a way to filter out distractions and focus on what you've determined to be most important. A daily intention can also guide decision-making, allowing you to commit to those endeavors aligned with your intention. When you use your intention as a barometer for your success, you are more likely to feel satisfied at the end of the day.

What do you believe are the most important outcomes of your work?

How could you use those outcomes to set an intention for your work?

What would constitute success for you as an educator?

How could you set an intention that allows you to define success for yourself?

Area 3: Leading and Following

Like student–teacher relationships, developing strong relationships has intrinsic value for both principals and teachers. Relationships between principals and teachers influence student learning through a more positive school culture, greater teacher effectiveness, and lower teacher turnover. Just like students, teachers thrive in schools where they feel safe, seen, and stretched. Like any strong relationship, principal–teacher relationships require communication and trust. Teachers can't control what principals bring to the relationship, but below are some reflective questions for teachers who wish to build stronger relationships with their school leaders.

How can you contribute to better communication between school administrators and teachers at your school?

How can you contribute to greater trust between school administrators and teachers at your school?

How can you embody the characteristics of a leader at your school, regardless of your title or position?

Notes and Works Cited

p. 124 Ward, D. (2014). *Teaching with the end in mind: A teacher's life history as a legacy of educational leaders*. Proquest Dissertations and Theses Global.

p. 124 Duhigg, C. (2012). *The power of habit: Why we do what we do in life and business*. Random House.

p. 126 Ravitch, D. (2013). *Reign of error : the hoax of the privatization movement and the danger to America's public schools*. Knopf.

p. 128 Barnett, K., & McCormick, J. (2004). Leadership and Individual Principal-Teacher Relationships in Schools. *Educational Administration Quarterly, 40*(3), 406–434.

12

Lessons on Impact

The temperature was forecasted to rise throughout the day, so we dressed in layers and made the short drive to the Lakeland Downtown Farmers' Market. Brian left me and my pile of belongings in space 39 as he went to park the car. Almost a year into this project, I'd developed a routine for setting up my booth. First, I'd position the table with enough standing room in front, and I would put my notepad and pens within reach. Then, I would stuff a small pack of tissues into my pocket. Story collecting had become more familiar, and I found some strategies to lessen my anxiety. The story-collecting process is a bit like fishing; it requires both patience and hope. And despite my need for control, I'd come to embrace the unexpected nature of this research project.

I've been asked to describe what it's like when people share stories of their teachers with me. I'm not sure I can accurately describe it, but I can recognize it. A mix of emotions rises up, a combination of gratitude, joy, and the longing to recapture the feeling of being in that teacher's classroom. There are so few places where we feel deeply loved and supported by people who don't have to love us. A teacher's love is a validation of our worth and a confirmation of our potential. As we get older, we more fully understand the gift of a teacher's devotion and discretionary effort. The stories become more meaningful, and the feelings grow stronger over time.

DOI: 10.4324/9781003122029-13

I connect with the storytellers because I feel the same emotions in remembering my teachers. And hearing these stories has helped me reflect on my own teaching. I never expected to identify with so many people from different places and backgrounds. Through this project, I have come to understand that we were all once small, walking nervously into classrooms on the first day of school, hoping to be loved. If we were very lucky, we ended up in classrooms where we felt safe, seen, and stretched. Now, we get to carry those feelings in our hearts, perhaps not consciously aware of their importance until some researcher at a farmers' market asks us to share a story about a teacher.

Evidence of Impact

As I put my sign out, the woman in the booth next to mine was hanging paintings on a display board. She looked over. "I'm Shay. What are you selling?" I briefly explained my project as she walked closer. "Oh, I love that," Shay responded. "I wish all teachers understood how important they are." Then she began to tell me about Mr. Hall, the teacher who opened up a world of possibilities for her.

"I grew up in a rural area where most of us lived on struggling family farms," she said. "Nobody had the money to travel, so we didn't see much besides home, school, and church. I had never been outside of my home town until Mr. Hall's eighth grade art class field trip."

Shay explained that Mr. Hall had applied for a grant from a foundation supporting art education and received the funds to take a group of students to the Philadelphia Museum of Art. The museum was about four hours away, so they boarded a bus very early in the morning. "The sun was up by the time we pulled into the city," Shay remembered. "I just looked out the window in amazement. I had never seen such tall buildings and busy streets."

Shay recalled climbing several flights of stairs and seeing the magnificent columns in front of the museum. "Inside there were sculptures, paintings, and photographs. Many of them were created by famous artists we had studied in class, like Rodin and Picasso. I couldn't believe I was in the same room as these works."

Mr. Hall took the students to a nearby restaurant for dinner before getting back on the bus. "I loved the energy of the city," Shay said. "It felt so different from the slow pace of home. I realized there was a whole world full of interesting places for me to explore. I still love to travel, and I always visit art museums. Wherever I go, I pick up a postcard to send to Mr. Hall."

I told Shay that her postcards offer something rare and wonderful to Mr. Hall: evidence of his impact. This project has demonstrated that most people remember at least one teacher with great affinity and appreciation. But people are busy, and former students don't often take the time to let their teachers know about the impact they made. A heartfelt note or a message on social media is a sweet validation. These messages are inspirational for all who read them, but they also offer something else—information about what makes a teacher memorable. If teachers understand what makes an impact, we can do more of it. And we can do it intentionally.

The desire to serve students better leads teachers to search for impactful practices. Discussions about impact often include the work of researcher John Hattie, who is known for his meta-analyses around influences related to teaching and learning. Dr. Hattie strove to identify those teaching practices which are most effective. He found the average effect size for all the influences he studied to be .40, which he calls a hinge point. Therefore, those who use his work as a guide advocate for implementing practices found to produce better than average results. It's tempting to assume that being an effective teacher simply requires implementing the teaching practices with effect sizes over .40. Dr. Hattie's work appeals to educators, in part, because it seems simple and prescriptive. However, even Hattie himself cautions against oversimplifying his findings. The way these practices are implemented matters. Context matters, and the unique needs of students matter.

The gift of Dr. Hattie's work lies in the reflection it generates. Impactful teachers do reflect on their practices, and they look for evidence that the strategies they are using are working for students. They talk about learning and evidence of learning with their students. Having spent years observing in classrooms, I am not a proponent of one-size-fits-all approaches. I've seen impactful teaching done in rooms with flexible seating, and I've seen impactful teaching done with students sitting in rows. Teaching practices aren't implemented in a vacuum; they are implemented with people. And people are complicated. Teacher impact is far too complex to be easily quantified or captured with a checklist.

Teachers get mixed messages about what constitutes impact. For decades, policy makers have tried to narrowly define it, suggesting that it can be quantified and measured. In Florida, the state where I've spent most of my career as an educator, the Department of Education has created a long and complicated definition of teacher impact. The conferring of the title "High Impact Teacher" is based on something called a covariate adjustment model, a statistical model that attempts to control for the influence of multiple variables. In this case, the variables include a range of student characteristics, all of which defy quantification. In Florida's model, three years' worth of a student's test scores are entered into a calculation (way too long to include in this book) and compared to the student's expected score. The result is a number that is supposed to represent the teacher's impact on student learning.

Not only is this process convoluted, it excludes much of what students would identify as teacher impact. I've collected 276 stories and not one person has ever mentioned test scores. Searching for better, broader definitions, I came upon Bill Smoot's explanation of the education triad, comprising the teacher, the student, and that which passes between them. What passes between a teacher and student happens in the context of their relationship, and the relationship is a catalyst for learning. According to Dr. Smoot, effective teachers care deeply about their students' emerging understanding of the content. They care about their students' needs as learners and as people. This caring is not just a feeling, it is manifested in action. Impact, then, is derived from what teachers do in the interest of their students.

Impact is grounded in the many and varied ways teachers help students feel safe, seen, and stretched.

Imperfect Impact

The crowd at the market grew larger as the morning grew later. I had collected several stories by the time Mathias arrived at my booth. "I'll bet you hear a lot of stories about perfect teachers," he said. "My favorite teacher was not perfect, but that's why he was my favorite."

I was excited to hear Mathias's story because I'd been worried about teachers misunderstanding my data, thinking they need to be impeccable in order to make an impact. I view the stories I've collected as a highlight reel, showing the best and most impactful moments. Over time, students forget about the insignificant moments. Their memories are what remains after the mundane is sifted away, leaving only the significant moments to be carried and recalled when prompted. It is unrealistic to think that every moment in a classroom could be significant. And it is unhelpful to think that missteps and mistakes do not occur in every classroom. But with awareness and intention, teachers can use these as teaching tools. Mathias's story illustrates the power of imperfect moments.

"As a kid, I had a bad temper and a short fuse," Mathias began. "I often felt angry and frustrated. I grew up in a home with substance abuse; there was constant yelling and fighting. School was my safe place, even though I often got in trouble." Mathias admitted that in most classes, he would get sent to the office or sent home when he acted out. That changed in Mr. Byron's fifth grade class. "When I got angry, he would quietly tell me to go get a drink of water then come back and talk to him. He asked me questions and listened in a way that showed he really cared. He had a way of breaking through my anger and calming me down."

Mathias recalled a day when he got frustrated and broke another student's pencil. "It was the one time Mr. Byron lost patience with me. He said, 'What is going on with you? You have to stop doing this. What do you think is going to happen when you get to middle school?' Instead of talking, he just asked me to move to a seat in the back of the room. I felt ashamed and rejected, even though I knew I deserved it. I quietly got on the bus after school without my usual high five and pep talk from Mr. Byron."

Mathias told me he was surprised to see Mr. Byron standing on the bus ramp the next morning. "Mr. Byron asked if he could join me for breakfast. As we sat together in the cafeteria, my teacher explained, 'I owe you an apology. I am really sorry that I let you down yesterday. I was impatient and didn't listen to you, and that wasn't right.' I was shocked. I told Mr. Byron that no adult had ever apologized to me before. He looked at me for a minute, and then he said, 'I think you are probably owed many apologies.' We both knew that was true."

Mathias revealed the significance of that moment with Mr. Byron. "I was always being asked to apologize to others, but being on the receiving end of a sincere apology was a changing moment in my life," Mathias said. "We agreed that I would replace my classmate's pencil and offer a sincere apology of my own."

Mathias's story is a beautiful reminder that even the closest relationships have conflict, and even the best teachers make mistakes. Author and shame researcher Brene Brown is familiar with the propensity for perfectionism in teaching. Being a role model for students can lead to a need to present oneself as perfect. Perfectionism is born of the fear that we will be seen as we truly are and won't measure up to the expectations of others. While perfectionism protects us from being seen, it keeps us from real connection. It stifles our relationships. The only way to create meaningful relationships is to show up as our authentic selves, flaws and all.

Children who see the adults in their lives making mistakes are more accepting of their own mistakes. When we embrace our own imperfection, we give students permission to be imperfect too. Yes, our students are always watching, and we can allow them to see us use our mistakes as opportunities to learn and grow. We teach powerful lessons when we talk openly about our mistakes and when we seek ways to do better next time. Vulnerability is transformative in the classroom, and it begins with us. Our students don't need perfect teachers; they need real teachers who show them how to live authentically in an imperfect world.

A Legacy of Impact

The ties between authenticity and impact had been on my mind in the weeks leading up to my time at the market. I'd recently attended the funeral of a mentor, Dr. Earl Lennard, whose guidance was indispensable during my decades as a teacher and administrator. He had risen through the ranks in the nation's eighth largest school district, from history teacher to superintendent. Dr. Lennard was raised on a farm and always saw himself as a farmer. He had a knack for communicating profound life lessons in simple, memorable ways. When his daughter, Missy, and I were opening a new school and dealing with a barrage of urgent issues, Dr. Lennard advised us to just "shoot the alligator closest to the boat." His wit and wisdom were always delivered with care and compassion. He made everyone he met feel safe, seen, and stretched.

As I walked into the funeral, I realized that Dr. Lennard's legacy is not just the school that bears his name. His legacy lives in the hearts and minds of the people who crowded into the auditorium to pay their respects. One by one, colleagues and friends stood at the podium to share a story about the impact Dr. Lennard made on their lives. Jim Hamilton, who had been his teaching intern and eventually his deputy superintendent, spoke of a day early in their relationship. Dr. Lennard wanted Jim to see the conditions in which some of their students lived, so he drove Jim through a community mainly inhabited by migrant farmworkers, and they stopped on Railroad Street. Jim said, "Earl pulled over by a small house with a ditch of standing water in front, a breeding ground for mosquitoes. Near the ditch was an open window, no screen, with a baby's crib in view."

Jim remembered the words Earl said to him. "There's a baby in that house. Our job is to make life better for that baby. When you see these kids in school, remember you have to help them get out of that situation through an education." Jim never forgot Dr. Lennard's words, and those words shaped his life's purpose. Together, the two of them made life better for countless students over their decades of service.

Dr. Lennard's impact is no accident. Always a farmer, he cultivated his legacy with intention and care every day. Because of our positions of influence, educators are well positioned to create powerful legacies. As Dr. Lennard modeled, leaving a legacy requires us to consider how our daily actions and interactions have an impact on the future. It is simultaneously present- and future-focused. Legacies are built when we enact our personal missions while also helping others fulfill their purposes. It is both self- and other-focused. Leaving a legacy is an individual pursuit, but it benefits the people and communities we will eventually leave behind.

Dr. Lennard's funeral helped me understand that legacies are comprised of stories. Each person in the crowd that day had a story about a moment when he impacted their lives. Stories, like those shared about Dr. Lennard, are reconstructed as we tell them. We select details and continuously reinterpret meaning. With distance and reflection, we make connections between a past experience and our present lives. Often, the stories we tell contain messages that have become guideposts for our lives. Sociologist Andrew Abbott has identified the power of turning points in the stories we tell. During a turning point, we find ourselves in a state of struggle, despair, or unknowing. We then encounter someone who responds to this need while demonstrating care and commitment to our growth. Because of the intervention, change occurs and we begin a new trajectory. The more we assist others through turning points, the richer our legacies become.

Many of the stories I've collected center on a turning point. According to Dr. Abbott, turning points are both ordinary and rare. They stem from seemingly common actions on the part of a teacher, but students experience very few of these moments over the course of their years in school. We can't force a turning point, but we can create the conditions under which they are most likely to occur. Turning points happen in classrooms with high levels of trust and acceptance. They happen when teachers communicate enthusiasm and commitment. And, turning points occur in the presence of high expectations. Turning points are serendipitous to some extent, when the right words or actions are offered to the right student at the right time. However, turning points are most likely to occur when students feel safe, seen, and stretched. When we are intentional about the way we connect with students and what we expect of students, we build legacies of impact.

A Search for Meaning

The afternoon sun emerged from behind the clouds, heating the brick street and sending the remaining patrons searching for shade. Looking due south, I could almost see the shop where I had purchased my sign from Justin nearly a year ago. I began this project with the intention of answering a question: *What do teachers say and do to make a lasting impact on their students' lives?* The answer seemed so deep and complex, and I knew I could not answer it completely, certainly not succinctly. Yes, a framework had emerged from the data, but there are as many ways to help students feel safe, seen, and stretched as there are teachers. Feeling overwhelmed, hot, and tired, I decided it was time to call it a day. And that was the moment Ellen approached on her scooter.

As Ellen shared her memories of Mr. Dillon's speech class, I felt a sense of clarity. She recounted his cancer diagnosis, his promise to return, and his commitment to teach despite the pain. Ellen's words offered me assurance that the stories students tell collectively paint a comprehensive picture of teacher impact. These stories make the abstract notion of impact more concrete. There are many paths to impact, but they all center around the way teachers make students *feel*. Ellen felt safe, seen, and stretched in Mr. Dillon's class; the same feelings hundreds of other storytellers had conveyed.

Ellen's words confirmed how small moments in a classroom can make a big impact on students' lives. "I have experienced many challenges over the years since I was in Mr. Dillon's speech class," Ellen said. "When I start to feel sorry for myself, I remember the way he showed up every day, fully committed to teaching.

"Mr. Dillon has been my model of perseverance and strength. He is proof that it is possible to keep moving forward, even when obstacles get in the way. I appreciate how much he taught me—about giving a speech and about living a purposeful life." Her words are a testament to Mr. Dillon's legacy.

As Ellen traveled down the street and out of sight, I thought about Mr. Dillon, who stood in front of his students with a frail body and an indomitable spirit. He inspired Ellen in those moments, and the memory has continued to inspire her for decades. Mr. Dillon's significance in her life has grown with time and distance. And since Ellen shared the story with me, Mr. Dillon has become a source of inspiration in my own life. Now I share his story so that it may encourage others.

Perhaps teacher impact is really about the way imperfect teachers, through intention and effort, help imperfect young people learn to live happier, healthier, more fulfilling lives. By doing so, teachers not only impact a student's life but every life that student touches. Impact exists in ripples. Never underestimate the power of small moments in small classrooms. Those moments grow in significance over time, shaping lives, shaping families, shaping communities. What happens in classrooms between students and teachers has the power to shape the world.

I left the farmers' market with a head full of stories and a heart full of gratitude for all of the teachers I knew—those who had stood before me and those I encountered through the memories of their former students. Through this research, I endeavored to add to the body of knowledge about teaching and to elevate the profession. What I did not anticipate was the way the research would affect my life. Being conscious of the importance of helping students feel safe, seen, and stretched made me a better teacher. But it also made me a better parent, spouse, colleague, and friend. Inspired by the stories participants shared, I set an intention to make a positive impact on everyone in my life. Holding the awareness of that intention has influenced all of my actions and interactions. Perhaps this is the best way to honor our teachers—to be mindful of our own impact.

The bonds that are forged between teachers and students are rarely replicated in other contexts. Imagine what would happen if we all approached our relationships with the intention of helping others feel safe, seen, and stretched. Turning ordinary moments into moments of extraordinary impact is what teachers do every day in a million different ways in classrooms around the world. When students experience these moments, they are changed. This project may have yielded as many questions as answers, but there is one thing I know for sure: the impact of our teachers is indelibly woven into the fabric of our lives.

Applying Lessons on Impact

Making an impact can happen serendipitously, when we do or say the right thing at the right time. But making a consistent impact happens with intention. Being mindful of how our actions and interactions affect our students is a necessary practice. When we know what makes an impact, we can do more of it. Below are three areas for reflection on impact.

Area 1: Defining Impact

Teacher impact is often narrowly defined as an increase in student achievement test scores. While test scores may provide some evidence of student learning, teacher impact reaches well beyond scores. Impact encompasses the many ways teachers facilitate better academic, social, and emotional outcomes for students.

How do you define your impact as a teacher?

Using your definition, what evidence of your impact can you identify?

Area 2: Leaving a Legacy

Your legacy is grounded in the impact you make on the lives of others. Legacies are built intentionally by considering how present actions and interactions will shape the future. We will all leave our professional work behind one day. It's never too early to begin thinking about the legacy that will live on after we are gone.

How do you want to be remembered?

What stories do you hope will be told?

What impact do you hope to have made on the people you have encountered?

Area 3: Journaling for Impact

Impact happens when students feel safe, seen, and stretched. It comes from knowing our students and understanding their needs. Consider keeping a journal with a separate page for each student. Record any notes that may be helpful in strengthening your relationships. Below are some reflective questions to guide you.

What is this student's experience in this classroom?

How does this student feel about me, about classmates, about learning?

What does this student need to be fully engaged in this classroom community?

What are this student's goals and dreams?

What support does the student need to reach those goals and dreams?

Notes and Works Cited

p. 135 Hattie, J. (2009). *Visible learning: a synthesis of over 800 meta-analyses relating to achievement*. Routledge.

p. 136 Smoot, B. (2010). *Conversations with great teachers*. Indiana University Press.

p. 138 Brown, B. (2010). *The gifts of imperfection : let go of who you think you're supposed to be and embrace who you are*. Hazelden.

p. 140 Abbott, A. D. (2001). *Time matters : on theory and method*. The University of Chicago Press.

Epilogue

Many changes occurred while I was fashioning this research journey into a book. Brian and I left our beloved Lakeland and our positions at Florida Southern College to pursue new opportunities as faculty members at Appalachian State University. We traded our downtown bungalow for a cottage in the woods. The mountains, constantly transforming with the seasons, remind us that change is inevitable.

Cailin successfully navigated her first year as a teacher. She experienced a range of emotions: idealism, confusion, excitement, frustration, elation, and exhaustion. She started the second year a little wiser and more skilled, and she continues to grow. Her box of notes, drawings, and other tokens of affection from students buoys her through the difficult days.

The Chalk and Chances project continues to evolve. I still collect stories about the teachers people remember. I share the stories through the Chalk and Chances website and through presentations about the project to audiences around the world. I remain in awe of the remarkable ways teachers shape students' lives.

The best part of sending this book out into the world is the opportunity to connect with readers. I treasure your thoughts and your feedback. You can engage in the conversation through social media using the hashtag #SafeSeenStretched. Or you can engage with me directly on Twitter and Instagram, @JulieSHasson.

DOI: 10.4324/9781003122029-14

I have been blessed to be in the company of so many amazing teachers throughout this journey. Although you and I may never meet in person, dear reader, I want to thank you for the difference you make in the lives of others. Your effort to help the people you encounter feel safe, seen, and stretched is what makes the world a better place.

For Product Safety Concerns and Information please contact our
EU representative GPSR@taylorandfrancis.com Taylor & Francis
Verlag GmbH, Kaufingerstraße 24, 80331 München, Germany